D0432214

DATE DUE

JUN 06

AUG 24 08

GAYLORD			PRINTED IN U.S.A.

Scrapbooking Sports

Celebrating Your Family's Sports Adventures

Kerry Arquette & Andrea Zocchi

Dad is an avid
fisherman and loves
to share that with
Anna. I love this
picture of the two
of them

FISHING

cantata books   LARK BOOKS

JACKSON COUNTY LIBRARY SERVICES
MEDFORD, OREGON 97501

EDITOR
Kerry Arquette

ART DIRECTOR/DESIGNER
Andrea Zocchi

COVER DESIGN
Barbara Zaretsky
Andrea Zocchi

CONTRIBUTING WRITERS
Terri Bradford
Lois Duncan

EDITORIAL SUPPORT
Anne Stroud

HAND MODEL
Erin Foley

We'd like to thank

our families and dear friends, including the crew of Lark Books, who supported us during the creation of this book. Thanks also to the artists who allowed their creative visions to flood these pages.

Created and produced
by Cantata Books Inc.

P.O. Box 740040
Arvada, CO 80006-0040

www.cantatabooks.com

10 9 8 7 6 5 4 3 2 1

First Edition

Published by Lark Books, A Division of
Sterling Publishing Co., Inc.
387 Park Avenue South, New York, N.Y. 10016

© 2005 Cantata Books Inc.

Distributed in Canada by Sterling Publishing, c/o Canadian Manda Group,
165 Dufferin Street, Toronto, Ontario, Canada M6K 3H6

Distributed in the U.K. by Guild of Master Craftsman Publications Ltd.,
Castle Place, 166 High Street, Lewes, East Sussex, England BN7 1XU
Tel: (+ 44) 1273 477374, Fax: (+ 44) 1273 478606, "email": pubs@thegmcgroup.com,
Web: www.gmcpublications.com

Distributed in Australia by Capricorn Link (Australia) Pty Ltd.,
P.O. Box 704, Windsor, NSW 2756 Australia

The written instructions, photographs, designs, patterns, and projects in this volume are intended for the personal use of the reader and may be reproduced for that purpose only. Any other use, especially commercial use, is forbidden under law without written permission of the copyright holder.

Every effort has been made to ensure that all the information in this book is accurate. However, due to differing conditions, tools, and individual skills, the publisher cannot be responsible for any injuries, losses, and other damages that may result from the use of the information in this book.

If you have questions or comments about this book, please contact:
Lark Books, 67 Broadway, Asheville, NC 28801. Tel: (828) 253-0467

Manufactured in China

All rights reserved

ISBN 1-57990-736-9

For information about custom editions, special sales, premium and corporate purchases, please contact Sterling Special Sales Department at 800-805-5489 or specialsales@sterlingpub.com.

Contents

There's nothing normal and everything extreme about it: you ski like a maniac!

Whistler is no match for your Double-Diamond-Daredevil SKILLS

Daredevil

EVEL KNIEVEL

AFRAID

DANGEROUS

MOTORCYCLE

STUNT

thomas

whistler AIR

S KI

Tia Bennett

Introduction

Sports are as much a part of our lives as scrapbooking and so it's natural that the two interests should somehow meet. And what better place than on terrific scrapbook pages that feature us, our favorite athletes, and sports venues?

Sports scrapbook pages can be as carefree as a pennant-waving fan or as powerfully assertive as a rugby scrum. They can showcase moments of fierce competition or those down times when players are caught on film at their most vulnerable—waiting for their turn to take the field or debating strategies with coaches.

Scrapbooking Sports is filled with terrific scrapbook art that will inspire you to create your own sport-themed pages. There are also ideas for scrapbooking the fans, the fields, historical sports photos, the wins and the loses, and even a special section encouraging you to get down-and-silly with scrapbooking fictitious sports.

So set aside your balls and bats, your golf clubs, your rods and reels, and all your other sporting equipment for just a while, and dive into *Scrapbooking Sports*. While the glory of that heart-lifting win may last only until the next inevitable defeat, and your visit to the ball field may last only until the smell of popcorn is finally licked off your fingertips, your sports scrapbook pages will last long after the roar of the crowd has stilled.

Enjoy!

Kerry and Andrea

SOMETIMES WE WIN

Once in a while there's a day when you wake
And you know that you never can make a mistake.
Your breakfast is all of the things you like most.
The jelly stays put on the top of the toast.

You're late for the school bus – it comes in a minute.
A seat by the window has nobody in it.
You get back a test, and it's marked with a star!
You run in a race. You're the winner by far.

You slide into home at a Little League game,
And everyone's cheering and shouting your name.
The sun is so bright, and the sky is so blue
That you know that the world was invented for you!

Once in a while it can happen that way
On a beautiful, wonderful, very good day.

Lois Duncan

SOMETIMES WE LOSE

The batter swung hard, and he hit a fly!
I watched that ball zoom into the sky.
I started to race to the place it would go,
Then I tripped on a rock and I stubbed my toe.

My shoelace broke, and I wanted to cry,
But that ball kept coming, and so did I.
Then, I stepped on my shoestring and fell on my face,
And watched the runner slide into the base.

I hated that runner! I hated the ball!
I hated the umpire who made the call!
I'd never believed I could feel so bad
'Til I looked at the stands, and I saw my Dad.

He was cheering and shouting, "Wow! What a game!"
And I knew he was proud of me all the same.

Lois Duncan

Scrapbooking Supplies

Time to shop! Oh yeah! Whether you're off to your local hobby or scrapbooking store, or are visiting your favorite online scrapbooking supply store, you're sure to be wowed by the wide selection of cardstocks, patterned papers, colorants, embellishments and other products available for sports scrapbooking pages. If you're looking for something specific, be sure to take along your photos so you can check out color combinations. And take along this book for inspiration as you fill your cart with fabulous scrapbooking products that are well worth cheering about.

Paper

Scrapbook paper is available in cardstock or patterns and in speciality papers such as mulberry and metallics. Buy by the sheet, or look for prepackaged papers that are designed to work together. Many manufacturers offer sports-themed paper with ball, or activity patterns, or scripts that highlight important aspects of the game or competition. Look for papers that are acid- and lignin-free in order to prevent photos and papers from yellowing and becoming brittle.

Colorants

Get even more creative by altering your papers and other scrapbook page elements with colorants. Paint brads, charms, frames and other elements to make them better coordinate with your paper and photos. Use paint or ink to create interesting patterns or to draw attention to certain portions of your artwork. Stamping inks can create complex customized patterned papers and page titles.

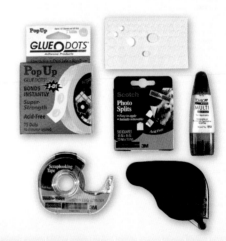

Adhesives

Scrapbooking adhesives allow you to place even the smallest elements on a page cleanly. Adhesives intended for scrapbooking are photo-safe, which means they will not damage your pictures over time. Look for liquid adhesives, photo splits (small sectioned pieces of double-sided tape), photo-safe tape, tape rollers and foam spacers.

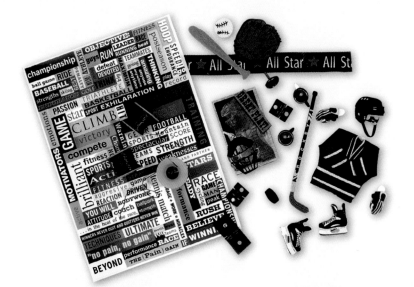

Embellishments

Eyelets, brads, stickers, die cuts and other embellishments with sports themes are widely available for adding decorative dash to sports-themed scrapbook pages. Mix them up with sports-themed or other patterned papers. Wrap elements in fibers or ribbons for extra flair and add a touch of sheen with metal frames or tags.

Scrapbooking Terms

Cropping: Cropping is the act of trimming photos to enhance the image by reducing extraneous portions of the shot. You may also wish to crop photos into rounded or other artistic shapes, or to crop around primary images and discard the rest of the picture.

Matting: Matting is the layering of photos or other page elements on a second piece of paper. Double and triple matting involves the rematting of the matted element on a third and fourth piece of paper.

Mounting: Mounting is the process of adhering photos and other page elements to your scrapbook page. Use photo-safe adhesives in order to reduce deterioration of papers and photos.

Embellishing: Embellishing is the decorating of scrapbook pages. You may choose to use stickers, stamps, fibers, metallic frames, brads, charms, buttons or other products.

Journaling: Journaling is the recording of written information on a scrapbook page. While you may wish to share whole stories and descriptions of your feelings, minimal journaling should include the names of those in the photos, the place and date.

Maria Kress

PRACTICE MAKES PERFECT

THEY SAY THAT PRACTICE MAKES PERFECT. WELL BEN THINKS SO TOO. WHENEVER DADDY HAS SOME FREE TIME BEN 'HITS' HIM UP FOR SOME PRACTICE TIME. HIS THROW IS GETTING PRETTY GOOD!

JUNE 2004

BEN

ANGELA MOEN

Maine Scrappers

4

Position: Serious Scrapbooker
Favorite Subject: Son   Stamps: Left   Cuts: Right
Blocking, Composition, Photography   Best Techniques: Creative Stitching, Color

MAJOR LEAGUE SCRAPBOOKING RECORD

Year	Album	Pages	AB	H	2B	3B	HR	RBI	AVG
1997	Baby	12	520	161	21	1	9	48	.310
1998	Family	24	141	37	10	1	1	13	.262
1999	Vacation	18	367	108	19	2	1	26	.294
2000	Toddler	26	168	57	8	1	1	21	.339
2001	General	32	337	102	11	3	4	24	.303
2002	Family II	30	367	108	19	2	1	26	.294
2003	Vacation	28	194	65	9	1	5	25	.335
2004	Sports	34	442	221	40	4	20	62	.500

Major League
Scrapbooker

Above scrapbooking statistics are not factual. All contributors to Curtain Books are excellent artists and we don't really keep statistics on them as that would be absurd. All contributors to Curtain Books are excellent artists and we don't really keep statistics on them as that would be absurd.

PLAY BASEBA

SCRATC

MACK JONE

DARRYL HAMILTON
NEW YORK METS® OUTFIELD

P
51
2005

DIAMONDBACKS™

MON. MAR. 31, 2003

MIKE PIAZZA / METS®   vs. CHICAGO (NL)

280
SEC

11
ROW

31
SEAT

Baseball

Stick and ball games are common among many cultures in the world; however baseball is unique to America. The game first became popular in the early 19th century and something about the ball-swatting, base-running game captured the hearts of fans who wanted to be "taken out to the ball game and the crowd" as often as possible. People continue to swarm ballparks across the country each spring to support their favorite amateur or professional teams, and some record those memorable moments on engaging scrapbook pages that strike home runs in the hearts of enthusiasts.

Tarri Botwinski

Cubbies

Stamped twill tape creates borders between multiple black-and-white and color photos on this page. The red and blue background paper is as American as apple pie. An interactive baseball on the lower right portion of the page opens to reveal hidden journaling.

T-Ball

For the young ball players featured on this page, the game is all about watching and waiting. Creamy white textured cardstock is torn and laid upon a vivid red background before being overlaid with stunning black-and-white photos. Definitions, strategically printed on a transparency, are secured with ribbon. The squared off title treatment works well with the blocked, layout design.

She Scores!
Continuity is created on this page through a well conceived and creative title treatment. The mesh and metal title tags emulate the chain link fence in the photos.

Melaina Varble

Cherie Ward

The Season

Patterned papers and cardstock ribbons are machine-stitched over cardstock to form the intricately pieced quilted background. A bold title and journaling strips join a stamped twill tape embellishment, supplying information about the event. The double-matted primary photo is strong enough to take on the complex background, supported by assorted other action shots and a colorful and creative picture of at-ready bats.

Some kids can throw. Some kids can field. Our kid can hit! Hitting is definitely Sam's favorite part of baseball, but the waiting to get his chance at bat proved to be too much for him this year. He is not the kind of kid who can stand/sit around for any period of time and well, there's a lot of that going on in baseball. We noticed that Sam was getting more and more irritable about going to games and finally, he admitted that he really hated playing. We didn't want to let him quit before the end of the season but for our sanity and his mood we let him. It seemed to be a huge relief to him, and he didn't seem to be upset by the fact that he would not receive a trophy. All he wanted to do was play with his friends, and once he was able to do that his outlook improved. But, at least we share his thrill in being able to send that ball flying!!

The Kid Can Hit

A young slugger takes his turn at bat on this great page. A graphic transparency overlays this focal photo, adding a text accent that pops the picture from the page. The photo is mounted with clips onto blue cardstock to match the model's uniform color. Inked wood and mixed media title letters, faux newspaper paper, ribbon and brown inked cardstock support the palette and theme.

Renee Foss

Baseball

Aged and layered baseball patterned paper and sepia photographs lay the foundation for this spirited baseball layout. Wide strips of torn paper create a border that adds texture to the clean lines created with matted photos and a vellum journaling block. Fibers, a metal title, and circle brads embellish the page while adding a touch of color.

She Scores!

While the photo of the batter should draw the eye because of its dominant size, it is the supporting photo that makes this page so special. Although neither model's face can be seen in the shot, the in-your-face position of the coach says volumes. You wish you could eavesdrop on the conversation.

Becky Thackston

Cubbies 2004

A photo frame made of stickers, plus a sticker tag and page border make this page something to cheer about. A running stitch around the word "baseball" adds character to the page, which can credit its greatest strength to the impish smile on the face of the model in the focal photo. Matted supporting photos add balance and a sense of the moment.

Tarri Botwinski

Create the decorative sticker photo frame

1 Apply a collection of sports stickers to a piece of cardstock. The stickered area should be slightly larger than the photo you wish to mount. Allow the stickers to extend beyond the edges of your cardstock.

2 Use a ruler and a craft knife to carefully trim the outside edges of the cardstock.

3 Mat your photo in the middle of the stickered frame and mount the frame on your scrapbook page.

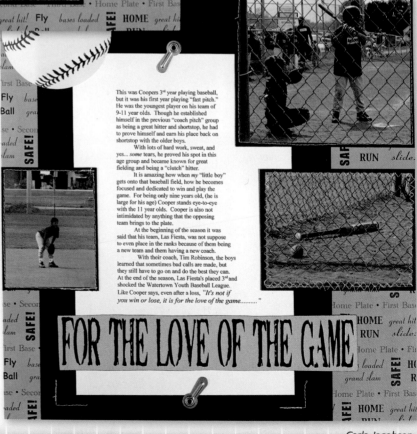

> ❝ *Good pitching will beat good hitting any time, and vice versa.* ❞
>
> *Bob Veale*

For the Love of the Game

A patterned paper background shouts out key baseball phrases on this baseball spread. The paper forms a backdrop for a terrific collection of action photos and a substantial journaling block. Varied stitching patterns decorate the edges of the mats and serve as photo corner decoration while supporting the rugged let's-get-out-there-and-play atmosphere.

This was Coopers 3rd year playing baseball, but it was his first year playing "fast pitch." He was the youngest player on his team of 9-11 year olds. Though he established himself in the previous "coach pitch" group as being a great hitter and shortstop, he had to prove himself and earn his place back on shortstop with the older boys.

With lots of hard work, sweat, and yes... *some* tears, he proved his spot in this age group and became known for great fielding and being a "clutch" hitter.

It is amazing how when *my* "little boy" gets onto that baseball field, how he becomes focused and dedicated to win and play the game. For being only nine years old, (he is large for his age) Cooper stands eye-to-eye with the 11 year olds. Cooper is also not intimidated by anything that the opposing team brings to the plate.

At the beginning of the season it was said that his team, Las Fiesta, was not suppose to even place in the ranks because of them being a new team and them having a new coach.

With their coach, Tim Robinson, the boys learned that sometimes bad calls are made, but they still have to go on and do the best they can. At the end of the season, Las Fiesta's placed 3rd and shocked the Watertown Youth Baseball League. Like Cooper says, even after a loss, *"It's not if you win or lose, it is for the love of the game.........."*

FOR THE LOVE OF THE GAME

Carla Jacobsen

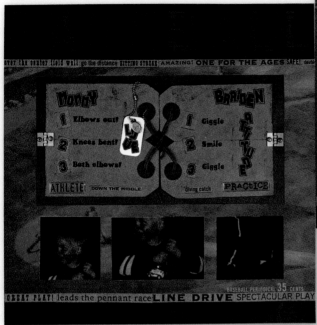

Sue Fields

Future All American

He may be a future All American, but right now this little athlete is just learning baseball basics. And he's being guided by a loving mother, whose advise is journaled on this page. Sticker borders run across the spread, and a complex assortment of tags, stickers and torn paper phrases are grouped to form a page title that is visually weighty enough to balance the large tilted focal photo (above). Hinged tags are manipulated and laced together to imitate a baseball glove (left).

> **Little League baseball is a very good thing because it keeps the parents off the streets.**
>
> Yogi Berra

Home Run Derby

This page mixes sass with outdoor sportsmanship and proves that sports are for people of all ages. The polka dot patterned paper speaks of the feminine power, as does its softly rounded edges. The inked edges and distressed title lettering celebrate outdoor fun.

Jessica Ulery

Rachelle MacIver

The Game of Baseball

Several different patterned paper strips and blocks are used to create the neutral base for the innocent black-and-white T-ball photos. Customized word labels applied to the photos denote moments of significance. Large letter stickers create a title that strides across both pages, linking them visually and creating continuity.

She Scores!

A sanded, painted, and inked child's board book is used as a photo album to hold additional pictures and journaling that could not be included on the spread. The booklet is held to the page (which has been reinforced from behind with a piece of heavy cardboard) with black elastic bands.

She Scores!

A portion of a real baseball is used to embellish the lower left corner of this stellar page, lending a feeling of realism, as well as dimension to the art.

Misty Posey

Fight it Out

Haphazardly applied paint decorates an angled red cardstock block that is adhered to playful plaid patterned paper on this fight-it-out page. Paint is applied to a real baseball's stitching and then rolled across a printed transparency to create a one-of-a-kind playful accent around the page title. Stickers and distressed stencils round out the picture.

Create a Rolled Baseball Seam Pattern

1 To create a seam pattern, lightly roll a baseball or softball across an ink pad. Or pour a small amount of paint into a shallow container and roll the ball through the paint. Roll the ball across a piece of transparency. Allow the ink or paint to dry before mounting the transparency on your scrapbook page.

Renee Foss

Go A's

An array of compelling photos are made even more interesting when slipped under negative transparencies, as seen on this page. The large focal photo sums up the team experience, while the smaller shots step out the day's action. Embellishments include a stenciled letter, tags, ribbon, and journaling on a transparency set with brads.

Play Ball

Sliding into home base is a dirty job and this page captures that dusty maneuver with an earth tone monochromatic palette. The baseball definition in the center of the page is created by scanning a sticker. The image is printed on a transparency and then mounted on brown cardstock before being attached to the page. The same sentiment appears on the partially displayed block on the left side of the layout. Photos are matted on heavily-inked cardstock. The "Play Ball" journaling block is stamped and slipped under the lower series of photos.

Shawna Martinez

Missy Crowell

All American Baseball

Monochromatic cardstock and striped papers are inked, crumpled, and torn to give texture and an old-world feel to complement the sepia photos featured on this spread. Sticker phrases define the topic at a glance, and the journaling is written in an off-beat newspaper-editorial fashion.

Teresa Brada

Baseball Is Life

Patterned paper recedes, allowing an action photo to steal the show. The red-matted focal shot is mounted with tiny hinges. Journaling appears underneath.Two small supporting shots are showcased inside negative strips. The creative title is built with a "Baseball" pennant, sticker words and a "Life" charm.

Play Ball

Large black-and-white photos with a contrasting colored photo are used on a striking base of cardstock covered with large mesh, lightly sanded striped paper and a painted title. The playful use of a mitered square paper border is adorned with star eyelets to reiterate the lightheartedness of the boy's take on the game.

She Scores!

The photos on this spread rack up points by capturing the all-boy personality of the model. Closely cropped photos draw the viewer into a one-on-one relationship with the ball player. The single color image adds a pop of color to the palette.

Tisha Mccuiston

She Scores!
The striped paper might have been mounted to the green background horizontally, but the vertical stripes help draw the eye from earth to sky, creating a greater sense of awe.

Play Until the Ball is Worn
This quick-and-easy page pulls its palette from the grass in the photo while a rectangle of striped paper, placed off-center, supports the eye-catching stance of the model. The page is completed with a powerful quote printed on a transparency and a date stamp.

Erin Sweeney

From the Color Guy
Baseball in the Early Days
According to the rules and regulations of the National Association of Baseball Players, established in 1866, sliding into base was legal. However, the maneuver was little seen until later in the history of the game. While runners often took extra bases on passed balls or when the ball was overthrown, it was not considered gentlemanly to slide—perhaps because of the potential danger of taking down an "adversary."

Janine van der Horst

As American as Baseball

Familiar baseball words on colorful strips supply the journaling for this happy sports page that features an action photo of sports heroes, matted and mounted on a colorful blocked background. The lower portion of the photo mat is cut and stitched to mimic the stitching on a baseball, adding to the page's theme. A small matted photo of tiny fans, mounted upon the focal shot, adds dimension. Star brads and tiny ribbons contribute to the festive air.

From the Color Guy
"Take Me Out to the Ball Game"

The song, written in 1908 by Jack Norworth, is said to have been inspired by a sign the author spied while riding a New York City subway train. The sign, "Ball Game Today," set Norworth thinking, and he jotted down the lyrics on a piece of scrap paper. The words were later put to music by Albert Von Tilzer and became a public favorite, sung by fans during the seventh inning stretch in almost every ballpark in the nation.

Baseball Time

Preprinted baseball-themed paper makes this spread easier to create than it looks, and mixing it with other patterns keeps the spread lively. The focal photo on the left side of the spread (above) is mounted over layers of vellum, printed paper and cardstock. The photo's edges are distressed for a rugged look. Brads and a ribbon-tied tag below the focal photo tie the page visually to the one opposite. A large ribbon with a mitt charm adorns the top of the right page. A handmade accordion album, embellished with another charm, metal-rimmed vellum tag and ribbon sports additional photos and journaling.

Lisa Bell

She Scores!

A homemade accordion album, created by folding and scoring a long piece of black cardstock, supports four additional photos and extensive journaling. It is a space-efficient way to include a collection of photos on a spread without overwhelming the artwork with images.

> **You gotta be a man to play baseball for a living, but you gotta have a lot of little boy in you, too.**
>
> Roy Campanella

Capturing the Location

As baseball continued to capture Americans' hearts, the field on which the game was played took on a romantic quality all its own. Glorified in poetry and song, "There used to be a ballpark where the field was warm and green, and the people played a crazy game with a joy I've never seen," ballparks are as much a part of baseball culture as the hotdogs and popcorn served there. Commemorate your favorite ballpark on a scrapbook page that captures the stadium's unique look and personality.

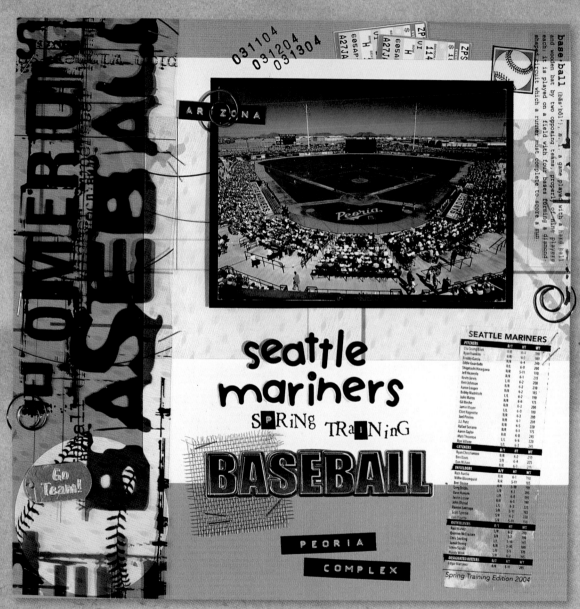

Trish Dykes

Mariners Spring Training

A postcard, used as a focal image, accentuates the vastness of the ballpark and supplies a shot of color on this black, white, and gray palette. The themed elements include a stapled transparency, stamping, stickers, label tape, and a Mariners' mini line-up (right bottom corner).

Deb Baker

Baseball Dreams

The littlest fan is all tuckered out, but he can catch up on events he missed by looking at this terrific spread. A collection of patterned papers, photos of the field, fans, and family are cropped and mounted on the spread. Ribbons, decorative slide mounts, colorful brads and staples embellish the artwork. Red embroidery floss is carefully stitched across photos at the top of the page, mimicking a baseball's seam. Additional stitching decorates the red mat under the focal photo. A terrific hand-made accordion album is attached to the page. Inside, are a series of great shots that simply couldn't fit on this full spread that commemorates a very full day.

What is both surprising and delightful is that spectators are allowed, and even expected, to join in the vocal part of the game...There is no reason why the field should not try to put the batsman off his stroke at the critical moment by neatly timed disparagements of his wife's fidelity and his mother's respectability.

George Bernard Shaw

Becky Fleck

Play Ball!

Title stencils, cut from antiqued brown and typographical papers, are set on red torn cardstock beneath a super ballpark photo on this fun page. A hand-stitched baseball and matching stitched photo mat further capture the baseball theme. Supporting photos balance the larger photo, while brads, page turns, and a tag embellish the layout.

Soccer

Spring, summer, winter and fall people of all ages and both genders pull on shin guards, shorts and cleated shoes to test their skills in moving a ball around human obstacles and into a netted goal. The high-paced running game knows no seasons as players move from grassy fields into heated facilities and back out onto groomed grassy fields. Even tiny athletes enjoy this energetic sport, and scrapbookers find their sideline seats allow them to click up-close-and-personal photos that contribute to powerful pages celebrating soccer sensations.

Kick It

Patterned paper, black inked dry wall tape, black cardstock and fiery photos come together on this spirited soccer page. Black brads, metal word plates and transparencies add dimension and make the page visually compelling. White label holders, painted a vibrant red, frame and call attention to smaller supporting photos.

Sue Fields

Discover Soccer

Gingham and printed ribbons soften this soccer spread, which calls upon gold and black cardstock to create a stark but dramatic palette. A collection of animated die cuts, stickers and journaling cut from patterned paper, convey a sense of fun well-suited to this young athlete's activity.

Kitty Foster

The country is full of good coaches. What it takes to win is a bunch of interested players.

Don Coryell ex-San Diego Chargers Coach

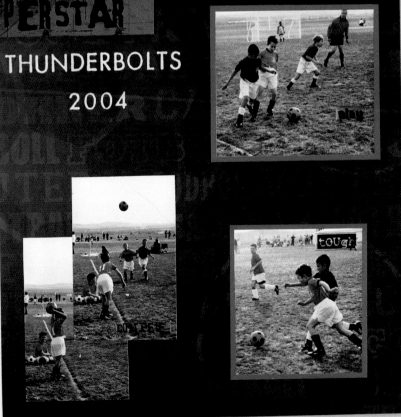

Thunderbolts

Just the right patterned paper becomes even "righter" when decorated with a printed soccer transparency. Word stickers and rub-ons supply the journaling for this spread that is big in color contrast and big in impact.

Leigh Fox

Having a Ball

Doris Castle

Soccer is a Kick

This completely digital page features a young soccer star against a field of grassy green paper. A journaled border holds down the left side of the page, set next to a faux "corrugated" green panel that houses the majority of the embellishments—tags, stickers, charms, metal letters and fibers. The journaling underscores the important aspects of the game including "passing," "teamwork," "rules," and, yes, "SCORING!"

From the Color Guy

Once Upon a Time

The earliest mention of a soccer-like game being played dates back to the Ts'in Dynasty in China (255 B.C.-206 B.C.). A game called tsu chu was played to celebrate the Emperor's birthday. Animal skin balls were kicked through a hole in a net stretched between poles. Similar games have been played throughout history in other countries around the world. Eskimos are said to have played the game on ice with balls stuffed with grass, caribou hair and moss. In England in the 12th century the sport was banned because the mobs who played it were out of control, but this didn't stop the game's growing popularity. In the Pacific Islands the game was played with coconuts, oranges and pig bladders.

She Scores!

What parent of a mini soccer player hasn't stood on the sidelines waffling between humor and frustration as her young athlete waffles between an interest in the sport and a need to socialize (or dig in the dirt or stare at the sky)? This photo captures the essence of the soccer experience perhaps more clearly than any goal-scoring photo ever could.

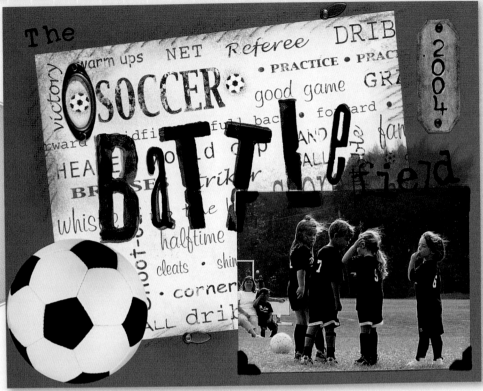

Krista Richardson

The Soccer Battlefield

A humorous tone is set with an engaging photo and a prominent title stamped across the patterned paper background on this page. The photo, accented with photo corners on green cardstock, as well as a clean soccer ball die cut ground the page.

Soccer

A young soccer player is going for the glory on this page that displays an effective use of color on a balanced layout. A cleanly matted action photo on black cardstock is mounted along with charming strips of green paper to a white background. The faux transparency negative strip holds a sequence of tiny photos that celebrate a series of slick soccer moves. The title block balances the multiple photos, and the text borders, at the top and bottom of the page, visually coral page elements.

"You'll always miss 100% of the shots you don't take."

SOCCER

soccer is a kick soccer is a kick soccer is a kick

Helle Greer

EVIDENCE

ALL I eveR NEEDED 2 KNOW I learned watching you play SOCCER

I press on toward the goal to win the prize for which God has called me...
Philippians 3:14

GOAL

our *Champion*

Spring 2004

Jessica Feliciano

She Scores!
The unique lower section of the page is created by layering a piece of mesh over a panoramic photo. The meshed photo is then mounted under a ripped window created in the patterned paper. For added interest, the edges of the ripped paper are sanded, curled and inked.

Our Champion
Hot orange patterned paper, layered with textured cardstock, makes this sizzling soccer page way cool. The photos are printed on fabric, which makes them look as though they have been painted. The decorated "evidence" folder opens to reveal journaling. A torn center strip exposes mesh mounted over a panoramic soccer photo. Journaling and brads complete the page.

Kick

What a kick this beautiful page is to admire. Lightly sanded green cardstock with coordinating rectangles of patterned paper, paper slide mounts, matted photos, and words create a game board look for this page. The elements masterfully guide the eye to the page title. The printed definition at the bottom of the layout serves as a platform for the winning artwork.

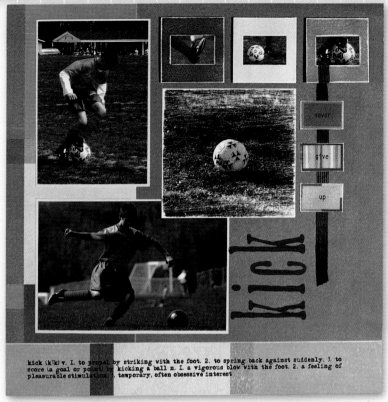

Dawn Burden

> *Football (soccer) is a game in which a handful of fit men run around for one and a half hours watched by millions of people who could really use the exercise.*
>
> *Unknown*

Soccer

A single sheet of patterned paper, cut into blocks, is all that is needed to create this quick and easy soccer page. Patterned paper blocks are mounted overlapping and beneath action photos. Letter and date stamps and a single rivet embellish the page.

Dana Crittenden

Kids, Cleats, Grass, Goals

Four matted tags, attached to soccer themed patterned paper with mini soccer brads, spell out the page title in a creative and fun manner on this terrific page. A photo-copied soccer patch embellishes the layout, which features a team portrait. Journaling completes the layout.

Madeline Fox, Team Photo: Gerald Porter

From the Color Guy

Play vs. Pounds and Problems (or) Where's Next Season's Sign Up Sheet?

Children and teens need 60 minutes of activity a day for their physical and emotional health. Even moderate physical activity (30 minutes of brisk walking or raking leaves, 15 minutes of running, 45 minutes of playing volleyball) helps.

According to a study done by the National Association of Sports and Physical Education, infants, toddlers, and pre-schoolers should engage in at least 60 minutes of physical activity daily and should not be sedentary for more than 60 minutes at a time except when sleeping.

Only about one-half of America's young people (ages 12-21) regularly participate in vigorous physical activity. One-fourth reported no vigorous exercise.

One quarter of U.S. children spend 4 hours or more watching television daily.

Childhood and adolescence are pivotal times for establishing patterns that prevent sedentary behavior among adults.

U.S. Department of Health and Human Services

Lessons in Sportsmanship

Sports are a learning experience, and these athletes are racking up the lessons, as witnessed by their expressions. The layout is simple, yet powerful. Black-and-white images and a substantial journaling block are given a bit of energy with small shots of blue. A sticker, and rub-on words embellish.

She Scores!

A series of black-and-white photos create clean and powerful pages. While color—especially bright colors— draws the eye, a black-and-white palette supports without fighting with photos for attention.

Lessons in sportsmanship...

Oscar and Luke, it's easy for me to tell you about sportsmanship and the lessons you will learn from the game. It is totally different to feel those lessons. Soccer is in your blood; both your dads still play and train every week, and it looks like you will follow them. It is so much fun when you first start playing roo ball. No scores are kept. You cheer for everyone, no matter how ordinary the shot. Each week you get to meet up with your friends, kick a ball around, score a few goals (or not), and celebrate with a bag of lollies from the canteen! Every game is a victory, win, lose or draw.

Then you get a little older, and the game becomes harder and more competitive. You are judged by goals scored, how strong your defense, by how well your team works together, by your commitment to the game. And that's when you learn that not everyone wants it like you both do; when the team fractures and you feel the sting of defeat in a final. After a season of hard work and training, of turning up each week no matter how bad the weather, and giving your all, it's over. The thing is guys...these are the lessons you have to learn. Under 11's semi final day - August 2003.

Jody Dent-Pruks

The Thrill of Victory

Soccer is all about action...and waiting...and action...and waiting. Capture all aspects of the game on a clean page that showcases a series of photos. Minimal journaling and a bold title contribute without detracting from the pictures.

Rachael Giallongo

Scrapbooking the Fans

Yes, throwing that touchdown pass is a heart-thumping experience. And so is performing that slide into home plate and executing the bicycle kick that drove the soccer ball so deep into the goal that the fans are still talkin' about it today. But being one of those fans who is doin' the talkin' can be just as much fun as performing the memorable deed. Some of us truly relish the chance to watch the parade pass by rather than trudging along with the horn or the flag. Fan enthusiasm contributes enormously to the fun for the marchers and spectators and deserves to be recorded on scrapbook pages that bring back the joy of being part of the roaring crowd.

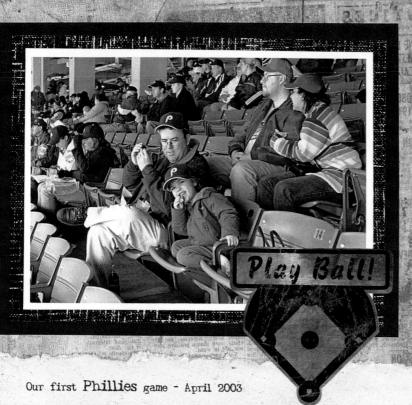

Play Ball!

Our first **Phillies** game - April 2003

John was so excited that Mary Rose was 3 and finally old enough that we could go to baseball games as a family. We got season tickets for 10 Sunday games - section 340, seats 13, 14, 15, behind 3rd base and under an overhang. The weather was cold this first game and we were worried she was getting antsy and wanted to leave. John got up and went to get hotdogs, and while he was gone the Phanatic came into the stands right next to us! I was taking pictures like crazy and Mary Rose was clinging to me for dear life, but she loved it! When John got back he couldnt believe he missed Phanatic, but Mary Rose decided she didnt want to leave and we stayed until the 7th inning.

Laura O'Donnell

Play Ball

A photo of a young fan is double matted and mounted on patterned paper, creating the focus of this fan-tastic page. A torn journaling block tells the story of the 3-year-old's initiation to the game. Light chalking and a the "play ball" sticker complete the layout.

She Scores!

While a closer crop might have focused attention more squarely on the father-daughter models, the wider crop sets them firmly in their environment. This supplies information about where the shot took place, the popularity of the game, the weather that day and other interesting facts.

Favorite Things to Do at a Baseball Game

Layered earth tone patterned papers and stamped sentiments join a stamped title on this page that is all about good times. The focal photo is double-matted and embellished with a ribbon-tied journaling tag. Dymo labels overlay the supporting images. Additional tags and ribbons, a typed "Take me out to the ball game" strip, as well as tiny floral embellishments complete the layout.

She Scores!

Tiny flowers, cut from an extra sheet of patterned paper, are used to embellish the artwork—a no-cost and no-fail idea for crafty scrapbookers on a budget.

Elizabeth Lee

BSU

A silhouette-cut image of a tried-and-true young fan is mounted on a sheet of sports-themed patterned paper. The patterned paper is stitched to an orange cardstock background. Stencil letters are painted, decorated with Dymo labels and matted on orange paper before being mounted atop stitched blocks to the background. A solid paper page corner works as a journaling block.

Shandy Vogt

Football

It all began in the 19th century when a frustrated British soccer player decided to scoop up the ball, tuck it under his arm and make a run for the downfield goal. A violation of soccer rules, yes, but a move that was so wild and wonderful it inspired other athletes to join in the fun, ultimately giving birth to the game of rugby, which in turn became American football. The game grew in popularity and now Sundays find fans across the country bundling up or nestling in to enjoy this sport.

Morry #85

The photo of a determined young athlete, is matted on brown cardstock that takes on a bit of the sport star's glow due to metallic rub-ons. Stickers, mounted on cardstock, are adhered to the background page and also suspended from the "M" bottle cap embellishment. Square metal letters and sticker numbers make up the title. All of the elements are supported by a muted patterned background paper. A booklet of additional photos is slipped behind the photo mat.

Mendy Mitrani

She Scores!
A sturdy brad connects a collection of supporting photos to the left side of the layout. When not being viewed, the photos are tucked neatly away behind the focal photo.

Lions

An aggressive stamped and painted page title is showcased on lightly painted cardstock. The inked library card holds a piece of paper indicating the player's name and number. It is stamped, distressed and embellished with a metal-rimmed tag. Letter pebbles and stickers support the layout.

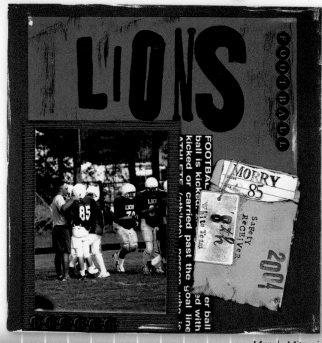

Mendy Mitrani

At the base of it was the urge, if you wanted to play football, to knock someone down. That was what the sport was all about, the will to win closely linked with contact.

George Plimpton

Lori Briggs

Football

Sepia photographs of a rough and tough day on the gridiron are matted and layered over brown football-themed paper and accented with blue cardstock on this sports page. Key phrases on a custom-printed transparency are highlighted with blue paint, and the transparency is further enhanced with stickers and white rub-on words. Clips, large distressed brads, and footballs add dimension.

100%

41

Laura McKinley

Tough

A textured and painted background creates a earthy platform for an incredibly powerful photo on this layout. The picture, framed within strips of medical tape, speaks volumes about the rough and tumble nature of the sport. A spray painted stenciled title, sticker words and twine tied through sturdy eyelets add an award-winning touch.

Create the textured background paper

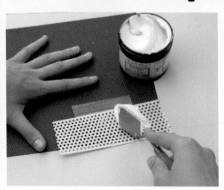

1 Lay a strip of drywall tape over a section of brown textured cardstock. Using a palette knife or your finger, apply a coat of pattern builder paste over the drywall tape.

2 While the pattern builder paste is still wet, carefully lift the drywall tape from the cardstock.

3 Allow the pattern builder paste to dry. Spray paint your desired color over the textured area.

Teresa Brada

She Scores!

A photo of the model's running feet is mounted beneath the "M" stencil on the lower right page. The angles within the stencil window and the angles of the model's legs create an arresting image.

Making the Moves

Textured red cardstock supports a collection of patterned paper blocks and strips, action photos and football-themed stickers on this dynamic spread. A painted and embossed "M" stencil, tape measure, stick pins and clips embellish the spread. The journaled transparency overlays the main photo on the left page, while a definition phrase for "achieve" runs vertically up the right edge of the same page. The crowning touch for this superior spread are the inked and embossed metal numbers hung by tiny fishing lures to form the player's number, "44."

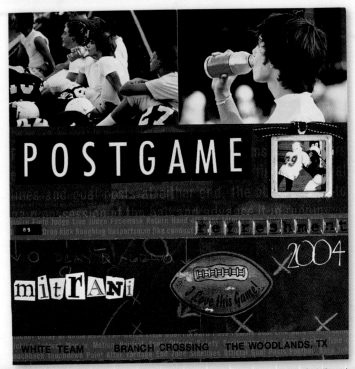

Post Game

Post game cool offs are an important part of all sports, offering time to chill and reflect, as seen on this page. Assorted strips of colored and patterned papers offer a background for two strong focal photos while a supporting image appears in a tiny frame. Journaling, created by mixed media embellishments, and a strong title complete the layout.

Mendy Mitrani

Angela Moen, Photo: Linda Sterns

She Scores!

Create your own journaled tag by typing the text directly onto a piece of paper. Print. Attach your tag with removable tape directly above the printed text. Run the paper back through your printer. Adorn with a ribbon.

Varsity Football

A single football photo is supported by a plethora of embellishments on this high school football page. Sticker letters and metal letters join a large football sticker on top of an island of textured cardstock and patterned paper. A metal-rimmed football tag, ball chain and layered papers hold down the lower left side of the page, joined by a journaled tag. Rustic ribbon and stitching add the final touches.

Football is Life

Football is a license for organized aggression, as seen on this page featuring a football license plate embellishment. A brown card-stock background supports a swatch of creamy cardstock over which are layered strips of grid patterned paper and a black paper strip. A title, label journaling, and an action photo complete the upper section of the page. The lower page features squares of inked patterned paper mounted on cream cardstock and embellished with the player's number, team name, and a mini license plate.

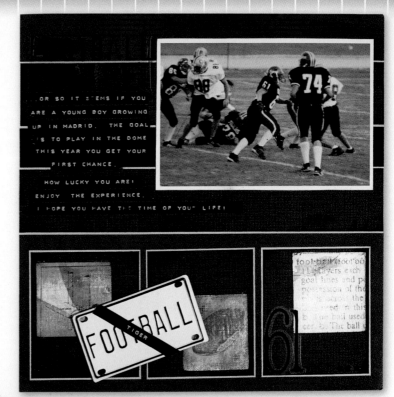

Peggy Nardini

Melissa Foshee

Pop Warner Football

Patterned paper blocks, a journaling block and neatly cropped photos form a clean geometric layout for this page. The monochromatic palette allows the photos to take center stage. A stamped ribbon title securely wraps around the cardstock, creating a clean upper edge.

Karen McKenzie

The Stance

The bold look of the enlarged photo on this page works perfectly with the large title letters which are mounted on red cardstock, below. Striped red and blue papers draw attention to the journaled transparency in the upper left corner. The word "STANCE" is highlighted with white paint on the journaled block, repeating and reinforcing the title.

> *In doing your work in the great world, it is a safe plan to follow a rule I once heard on the football field: Don't flinch, don't fall; hit the line hard.*
>
> Theodore Roosevelt

All About Football

A vibrant striped pattern, torn and mounted atop dark blue cardstock creates a mood for this football page. The stamped and painted off-set title is layered with black rub-on words. Bright orange photo mats complement the players' uniforms, while touches of brown cork, labels, tags and small embellishments trumpet team spirit.

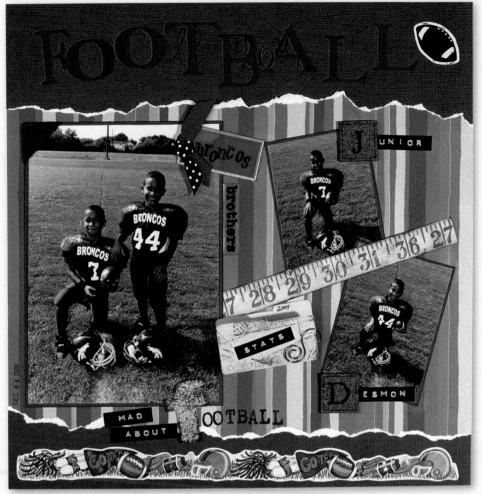

Sheredian Vickers

From the Color Guy
You're Yankin' My Chain (sports terms that really do exist)

To many, football is just downright confusing. So many bodies on a field. So much running about. And then there are all those terms, "bird cage," "pooch kick," "cornerback." Of course, in all fairness, football is not the only sport with its own vocabulary. Can you figure out what sports these terms are associated with? (answers on page 127)

1. flying hook to roundhouse kick, switcheroo swipe, airtrack, gainer, 360 gyro, cyclone, armada, handcuffs

2. grind, alley-oop, beni-hana, burly, madolly, lipslide, mongo, nollie, revert, ripper, roastbeef, sex change, swellbow

3. butt ending, back check, carom, crease lines, head deke, enforcer, passout, scramble, spearing, waffle pad

4. adloph, baby fliffus, back-in full-out, ball out barani, cat twist, kaboom, lazy back, lost move syndrome, randy

5. biter, draw, button, clean, frosty ice, hog line, in-turn, pebble, stone, takeout, blank end, bonspiel

6. attack au fer, balestra, beat, black card, coupe', glise', disengage, sabre, fuller, French grip, in quartata, hilt, flick

7. clout, chrysal, cresting, fletching, flo, anchor, jar, kisser button, matt, quarrel, Timber!, stabilizer, skirt, recurve

Basketball

In 1891, college physical education instructor, James Naismith, set out to dream up a sport that his young athletes could play during cold winter months in Springfield, Massachusetts. He decided to tape two boxes to bannisters at either end of a school gym and have his students shoot a soccer ball into the baskets. Before long, the boxes were replaced by peach baskets and, later, by netted metal rims. Today, hoops get their dose of action as young and old, tall and, yes, shorter players take turns dribbling across indoor and outdoor courts with dreams of glory in their hearts and the fans' commands to "shoot" ringing in their ears.

Meridith Watson

Dunk

Fabric, patterned paper and cardstock come together on this fun boy page. The blue crackle paper is created with a stamp. A sturdy stamped title, Dymo labels and an "all boy" button support the photos of the mini players. Manipulation of the photos renders some more opaque than others, adding an artistic montage. Colorful fabric ribbons adorn the photo mat.

Girlfriends

Feminine rickrack, pink polka dot ribbon and silk flowers adorn predominantly black-and-white patterned papers and a black-and-white photo, making this friendly page something to smile about. The photo mat is given a quick layer of pink paint and the acrylic "giggle" chip is painted pink and then swabbed down so the words can still be read. An assortment of pin buttons finishes off the design.

Rachael Giallongo

Rachael Giallongo

Teamwork

Polka dot patterned paper in team colors provides a whimsical mood for this all-about-team page. The oversized red photo mat, mounted over a ripped piece of white cardstock, provides space for journaling. Simple, but effective embellishments include metal letters, a Dymo label and a washer tag with the word "determination" dangling from the upper corner of the layout.

> **Be strong in body, clean in mind, lofty in ideals.**

Dr. James Naismith, the father of basketball

Ralonda Heston

...Nothin' But Net

A basketball-themed transparency is cut into sections and selectively mounted over patterned paper on this hoops page. Corrugated cardboard, torn and painted, adds both dimension and color to the layout. The tilt of the photos provides a feeling of movement. Dymo labels, twine, brads, and word washers that say "champion," "achieve," and "determination" complete the picture.

> *One man can be a crucial ingredient on a team, but one man cannot make a team.*
>
> Kareem Abdul-Jabbar, NBA Center

All Star

Layered coordinating patterned papers make this page a slam dunk. A matted photo is embellished with a journaled ribbon. Additional ribbon decorates the journaled tag, below. The title relies on letter stickers, while the journaling block hidden behind the picture is handwritten. Brads and a couple of shiny safety pins add dimension.

Angela Green

Sheridian Vickers

Hoops

Athletes start their training at a young age, and this little basketball player is no exception. This page comes to life with baby blue textured cardstock, complemented with red photo mats, buttons, ribbon and title letters. Patterned paper strips and a fancy buckle contribute to the fun.

Sarah Tyler

She Scores!
Catching an infant in motion can be tricky and calls for enormous patience. Be sure your camera is nearby and do your best to anticipate what is coming next. Go with the flow, because the shot you're sure will be a reject (the one where the model is simply tooooo close?) may be the shot that makes your page perfect.

A Boy and His Basketball
The orange basketball sets the palette for this terrific page, which features a model who is only slightly larger than the ball itself. Patterned papers, fuzzy fibers, journaled tags, and a title made from letter stickers all carry support the orange color palette. Black brads and an embossed black square clip provide contrast.

Daddy's Girl

Layered and inked cardstock and patterned papers support a three-point photo on this basketball page. The title is created with letter stickers. A "hoops" sticker, accenting sticker strips, and a tiny ribbon-tied tag complete this clean and simple layout.

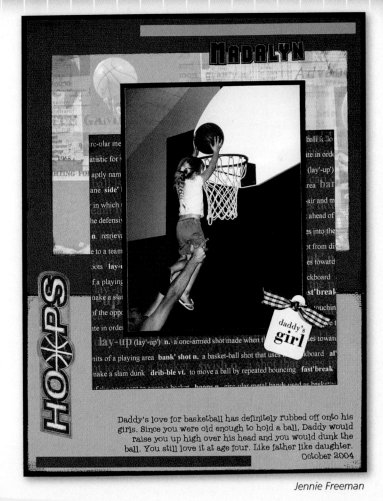

Jennie Freeman

From the Color Guy
Notable Useless Sports Facts That We Think Are Cool

- The largest attendance of live spectators for a sporting event is 10,000,000 at the 1994 Tour de France cycling race which took place over the course of 3 weeks.

- The largest professional sumo wrestler of all time was a Samoan-American named Seleeva Fuali Atisanoe who weighed 889 pounds.

- The longest time a basketball was spun continuously on the fingers of a single athlete was 3 hours and 59 minutes! AND the most basketballs to be dribbled at one time is 6! AND the most basketballs spun at one time on a specially built frame is 28!

- The longest ocean swim was performed by an Australian woman named Susie Maroney who churned her way from Mexico to Cuba, a distance of 122 miles. She broke a wrist in a storm and was stung by jellyfish, but kept on going.

- It took a Slovenian skier only five hours to ski from the top of Mount Everest to the bottom.

- The most people ever to complete a single marathon was 38,706 thousand. The event was the Boston Marathon in 1996.

- The term "bull pen," used to describe the enclosure in which baseball players warm up, may have been coined because it resembled cattle pens, or because it was originally located near a billboard featuring an ad for Bull Durham tobacco, or because it is where players sit and shoot the bull.

Facts recorded by the Guinness Book of World Records *folks and other reliable sources*

Lacrosse & Volleyball

Beyond the Big Four (baseball, soccer, football and basketball) exist ball sports that clamor to be scrapbooked on their own unique pages. Whether played in a backyard or gym or on a beach, volleyball is the sport of choice for hundreds of thousands of Americans. It shares popularity with high paced lacrosse. Capture the fun and fury of these sports on pages designed to showcase their intensity.

la·crosse (le krôs'), n.] a game in which two 10-member teams try to send a ball into each other's goal, each player equipped with a crosse for catching, carrying or throwing the ball.

She Scores!
Running the bold title vertically along the left side of the page allows room for the vertical photo to be enlarged to the max. The title block also serves as a page border, balancing the weight of the picture.

Lacrosse

When you've got exceedingly strong photos it is often best to opt for a minimalist style and let the pictures be the stars of the show, as seen on this powerful spread. An oversized stamped title, printed sports-themed transparencies—including a lacrosse definition—and a filmstrip border set with brads make this spread something to admire.

cradle   cradle   shoot

Helle Greer

Allison Landy

VBall 2004

Energetic yellow paper joins stark white and black papers on this paper-pieced background. Mesh is layered along the bottom of the left page, under the "V" stencil, and over a portion of a printed transparency on the right page. Photos, some with yellow-painted edges, are mounted on the background papers. Definition tags, painted with a wash of yellow acrylic paint, are mounted with clean white tacks. Epoxy stickers and Dymo labels rack up the points.

Serving and Setting

Balance is what makes this exciting page work so well. Patterned papers and cardstocks are layered to support the four photos. File tabs direct the eye to the stats strip in the center of the page. Clay phrases "determination" and "teamwork," as well as photo tabs, perform the same function, directing the viewer's eye toward the supporting shots. Letter stickers form the title. Journaling is typed on vellum before being mounted with decorative paper strips and brads. Additional brads, including a miniature volleyball provide embellishment.

Peggy Nardini

Capturing the Joy of the Win and Agony of Defeat

No doubt about it; winning is FUN! And losing ISN'T. But both winning and losing offer great opportunities to learn. Winners and losers alike discover that there is pride in giving it your best shot, whether or not you receive a trophy. Sports teach graciousness, sportsmanlike behavior and the concept that victors and those who lost the battle both deserve respect. Winning and losing moments shine a spotlight on the best qualities of athletes. Scrapbook them with pride and share them with others who are proud of your player's strengths off the field as well as on.

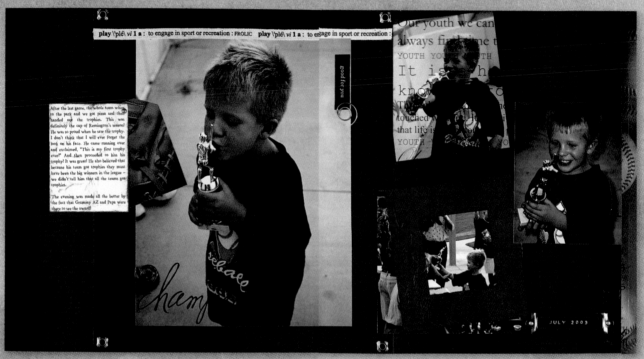

Syalynne Kramer

Champion

This young athlete's love of the game flows over to the love of his new trophy, as seen on this spread showcasing four photos. Printed transparencies, a journaling block, swirl pin and rub-on title word add their special qualities to the layout.

From the Color Guy

Inspiring Quotes on Winning

Wise men and women have shared their thoughts on winning. Use them on scrapbook pages and share them with the athletes you care about most.

"Winners never quit, and quitters never win."–Unknown

"If you think you can win, you can win. Faith is necessary to victory."–William Hazlett

"You can stand tall without standing on someone. You can be a victor without having victims."–Harriet Woods

"Let me win, but if I cannot win, let me brave in the attempt."–Special Olympics

"Accept challenges so that you may feel the exhilaration of victory."–George S. Patton

"If winning isn't everything, why do they keep score?"–Vincent Lombardi

From the Color Guy
Consoling Quotes on Losing

No doubt about it, losing isn't nearly as much fun as winning. But losing can teach us to view all of life's activities with a healthy perspective. Here are some great quotes about losing.

"Victory is sweetest when you've known defeat."–Malcolm Forbes

"The next best thing to winning is losing! At least you've been in the race."–Nellie Hershey Tullis

"Who has never tasted what is bitter does not know what is sweet."–German proverb

"Sometimes by losing the battle you find a new way to win the war."–Donald Trump

"The greatest test of courage on earth is to bear defeat without losing heart."–Robert G. Ingersoll

"I have missed more than 9,000 shots in my career. I have lost almost 300 games. On 26 occasions, I have been entrusted to take the game's winning shot—and missed. And I have failed over and over again in my life. And that is why I succeed."–Michael Jordan

Agony of Defeat

What a bummer losing can be. Just ask the young athlete on this page. Creamy cardstock and strips of varied patterned papers support the images of the model. A green envelope provides a surface for rub-on title words. Stickers, and chipboard embellishments offer hopeful, helpful thoughts.

Angela Moen

do what you love.

Chapter Two
Some Like It Hot, Some Like It Cold

Fishing Trip
Lunch - sandwiches, fruit, soda
Bait - night crawlers, minnows
life jackets
sunscreen
Gas & Toolkit

Scrapbooking Stuff
digital camera (flashcard)
notebook for journaling
plastic bags for memorabilia

Note: don't forget to take photos
f kids baiting hooks, Playing in
d and just being kids

Fishing

Wet and wild water sports offer a wide range of opportunities for athletes with an equally wide range of interests and dispositions. Some are called to dreamy days spent by a lake or pond, just waiting for that tug on the line that throws their heartbeat into high gear and their rod into action. Others enjoy tossing their line or their net into open waters and hoping for a fish so big that it will provide them with a story worth telling. No matter what and where you like to fish, capture the experience on peaceful or playful scrapbook pages.

Laura Ward

Fishing

Layers of patterned papers mix feminine chic with rugged colors for this serene father-daughter moment. The distressed-wood pattern of the papers is further weathered with sanded edges and subtle inking. The large stamped title with its irregular letters lends an antique-store finish to this well-worn page.

She Scores!

Tone down the newness of brads and other embellishments by covering them with a thin layer of acrylic paint. Softly sand dried paint for an antiqued look.

Take Me Fishing

An afternoon spent dockside with Grandma and Grandpa comes alive with texture and real fishing weights. Wood patterned paper mimics the wooden dock in the photos. Inked, torn and sanded corrugated cardboard look as if it's been recently washed ashore.

She Scores!

Construct a tempting title with a dash of symbolism. Model a title block after a sardine can, complete with a rollaway flap.

Lisa Sanders

Theresa Crawford

A Reel Treasure

Tender photos lie side-by-side to draw the eye and divide this page in half. The sepia tint enhances their quiet mood. The journaling block is slightly inked for an outdoorsy, masculine feel. A substantial journaling block at the bottom of the page tells the story of a shared fishing experience.

Gone Fishing

Patterned papers layered over mossy cardstock support photos that document a little fisherman's big catch. Journaling is printed directly on the cardstock background. Die-cut fish hang from a decorative brad, and others are grouped near a die-cut bag, overlaying a twill ribbon.

Jennie Freeman

The Color Guy

Fishing Quotes From the Wise and the Witty

"Give a man a fish and you feed him for a day; teach a man how to fish and you feed him for a lifetime."–Lao Tzu

"Give a man a fish and he will eat for a day; teach him how to fish and he will sit in a boat and drink beer all day."–Author Unknown

"Give a man a fish and he has food for a day; teach him how to fish and you can get rid of him for the entire weekend."–Zenna Schaffer

"Give a man a fish, and he can eat for a day. But teach a man how to fish, and he'll be dead of mercury poisoning inside of three years."–Charles Haas

Gone Fishing

Capture a quintessential father-son moment with rough-and-tumble papers and minimal embellishment. The fish, cut from patterned paper, and the "grain" of the wood patterned paper direct the eye to the focal photo. A splash of red in the double-mat pops the red shirt in the photo.

Tammy Brooks

Syalynne Kramer

Fish Kissin'

Boys will be boys, and this one likes to kiss his fresh catch. The distressed page design brims with details, including a delicate fish charm dangling from jute wound around a simple black frame. The bookplate does well to draw attention to the exclamation "yuck," a remark that those who aren't compelled to kiss a fish might well utter.

Holly Pittroff

Fishing With Poppy

One telling photo, overlaid onto paper with a distressed finish, is made all the more captivating by a simple brown painted frame. It conceals a fiber-accented tag with touching journaling describing the anticipation of a grandpa waiting for the day to teach his young grandson to fish. The printed overlay adds all the embellishment this page needs.

> **The charm of fishing is that it is the pursuit of what is elusive but attainable, a perpetual series of occasions for hope.**
>
> *John Buchan*

Fishing With Dad

Dramatic, enlarged photos create a sense of realism on this page and call for minimal embellishment. Strips of torn earth tone and plaid patterned papers echo the landscape alongside the water's edge. Letter tiles lend a youthful touch that any generation can appreciate.

She Scores!

If you love bottle caps but despise their bulk, simply lay them upside down and whack them with a mallet to flatten them.

Melaina Varble

Kimberly Billings

First Catch

This adorable and understated girly page perfectly showcases the pride of a first catch. The polka dot pattern is playful, yet the muted colors do not compete for attention with the photo. More feminine touches are provided with a delicate silk flower with a button center, rub-on stitched accents and a hint of ribbon.

She Scores!

The beaming pride on the model's face is so cute that the fish she's holding up might be overlooked if it weren't for the innovative framing technique to visually draw attention to the tiny catch.

Fishing

One thing is for certain—fun is the catch of the day, as seen on this page. The fiber fishing line embellishment takes the place of the portion of fishing pole that extends beyond the photo. The coordinating patterns of the bright paper help infuse the layout with fun, vibrant color, typical of a summer day.

Tammy Gauck

Deep-Sea Fishing

Cropped photos zoom in on the action-packed adventure of deep-sea fishing. To further enhance the action, slide mounts frame important visual points. The clean block design, coupled with the starch-white slide mounts, perfectly match the nautical theme.

> **It has always been my private conviction that any man who pits his intelligence against a fish and loses has it coming.**
>
> *John Steinbeck*

Deep Sea Fishing
Los Cabos, Mexico

Hot Sauce

Mahi Mahi

The day starts at 5:30am down at the marina. Rafeal rented his boat, Mucho Loco, with Captain Juan to us. We bought bait fish and started out. We caught 7 Dorado (Mahi Mahi) and released two. We spotted a Grey Whale and a school of dolphin. We were back at the Marina at 2:30pm.

October 1, 2004

Deck Hand

Angie Svoboda

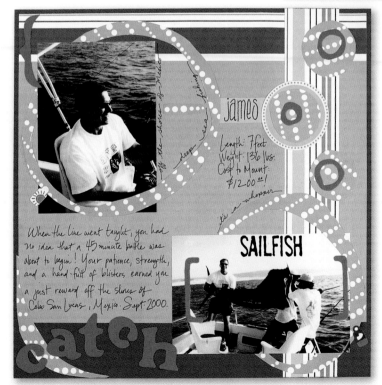

james

Length: 7 feet
Weight: 136 lbs.
Cost to Mount:
$1200 !

When the line went taught, you had no idea that a 45 minute battle was about to begin! Your patience, strength, and a hand-full of blisters earned you a just reward off the shores of Cabo San Lucas, Mexico. Sept. 2000.

SAILFISH

catch

Tia Bennett

Sailfish Catch

Striped patterned paper creates a strong border for this successful fishing page. The vibrant handcut title and funky circular and semi-circular shapes cut from bright orange and blue papers frame important portions of the page.

Boating and Water Sports

For some, a day on or by the water involves constant motion and high speed thrills. Whether on the deck of a speeding boat, or on skis in its wake; on tubes, rafts, or canoes, boating and floating are just plain fun. Capture those moments on pages that will call you back to the sun and surf in years to come.

Lake Nacimiento

Patterned paper that appears to have been sandblasted lends a foamy feeling to a lakeside spread. The fiber embellishment prevents the page from being visually flat and also echoes both the stripes in the paper and ripples in the water.

She Scores!

Improvisation can sometimes lead to genius. Here, that genius moment involves a soda-pop tab that serves perfectly as a buckle through which the colorful fibers are woven.

Janette Pettey

Get Your Feet Wet

This page glistens with totally tubular fun. The look of water is created by squeezing droplets of clear gloss onto the page and allowing it to dry. The photo mat glistens with more clear gloss, jazzed up with a hint of acrylic paint. A decorative metal strip, which is sanded and painted, separates the wet 'n' wild action shot from single-word descriptive journaling stickers.

Laura McKinley

Create a faux metal rope embellishment

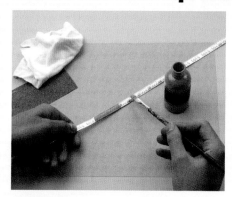

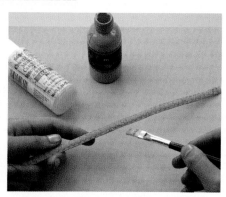

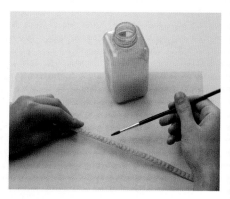

1 Lightly sand a narrow strip of metal. Clean the strip of dust and paint it your desired color. Allow to dry.

2 Paint the strip with a thick coat of crackle medium. When the medium dries apply the second layer of contrasting paint. Small cracks will appear, revealing the undercoat, as the paint dries.

3 Paint a clear top coat sealer over the crackled strip. Stroke in one direction and attempt to cover the strip in as few strokes as possible.

F+. Lauderdale 2004

Maria Gallardo-Williams

She Scores!

Cut down the time it takes to scrapbook a page by cutting down on journaling. Consider using oversized photo labels to supply necessary information. Add Dymo labels, and the job is complete.

Things That Start With B

Keeping with a lighthearted mood, bright and bold papers set the style with fun stripes and polka dot circles over orange cardstock. Label tape focuses the eye on the journaling, which in turn calls attention to the vibrant photos.

The Color Guy
Movie Sports Trivia

In 1959 the movie *Gidget* helped teens around the world fall in love with surfing. But other sports movies have had an equally strong impact on audiences. If you're one of those who prefers to watch sports in a comfy movie theater seat rather than on a hard ballpark bench, take this movie trivia quiz.. (Answers on page 127)

1. What was Kevin Costner's character's nickname in the 1988 movie *Bull Durham*?

2. In the movie *Cast Away*, Tom Hanks plays a character named "Chuck Noland," who develops an unusual relationship with an inanimate object. What was the object, and what was it named?

3. In a 1993 movie *Cool Runnings*, an Olympic bobsled team is featured from a very not cool (in fact, down right hot and humid) country. What was it?

4. In the movie *Rocky*, Sylvester Stallone's character drinks a concoction so nasty that anyone who saw the movie in 1976 is probably still gagging today. What was it made of?

5. What was the last movie in which Humphrey Bogart performed, playing "Eddie Willis," an unemployed sports writer involved with a boxer?

6. In the movie *The Bad News Bears*, the music from what famous opera makes the movie Bear-able?

7. In the 1980 movie *Caddy Shack*, the character "Grounds Keeper Carl," played by Bill Murray, destroys a flower garden while fantasizing about a Masters victory. What does he use to fricassee the flowers?

Becky Novacek

Mom, I'm Goin' Boardin'

The surf's up, and this young athlete is on his way out to meet it. A color palette of red, black, and cream provides the backdrop for this dramatic wall of vertical water photos. The title combines handwritten words and letter stickers. A large envelope with additional photos is embellished with script patterned paper, a photo, wooden letter blocks, a bookplate and ribbon.

Max

A simple burst of lime in this border takes this page to the vibrant max. More shouts of color exist in juicy strips of ribbon that enhance the model's life jacket. The creamy yellow of the patterned paper complements the model's skin tone.

She Scores!
Help direct the eye with savvy placement of an exaggerated photo corner. Add dimension with foam adhesive and direction by placing the corner so it points to the photo below.

Laura McKinley

Create a unique metal photo corner

1 Use a pair of decorative scissors to carefully cut a corner off of a metal frame.

2 With a rubber stamp and solvent ink, carefully stamp an image on the corner portion of the metal frame that you have removed. Allow the image to dry.

3 Swipe the corners of the stamped frame portion with watermark ink. While it's still wet, cover the ink with embossing powder and heat set.

A Picture Paints a Thousand Words

It's supposed to be fun, but that wind can turn a warm evening on the water into something a bit nippy, as seen on this blow-you-away page. A white frame draws attention to the model's face in the photo without obscuring the fun printed words that are part of the background paper. A vellum title, photo turns, and ribbons reinforce the border.

Sue Fields

Misfortune

Shots such as this are about as rare as shots of the caught-and-released fish that was "THIS BIG!" The tubing mishap and the witty journaling need no other embellishment on this page that takes its cue from popular posters that poke fun at the realities of the downtrodden.

Angie Svoboda

Solitary Soul

Printing color photos onto a transparency gives them a reflective quality that is both symbolic of the water sport, kayaking, and of the soul-nourishing experience of navigating the waters alone. Textured neutral background papers and purposely imperfect stamping add to the beachcomber feel.

She Scores!
A mixed-media title gets added shine when letters are dipped into extra-thick embossing powder. The shimmery letters look water-wet and sun-kissed.

Laura McKinley

Create a customized word tag

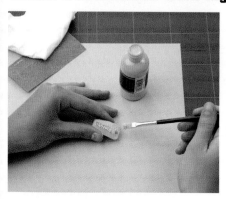

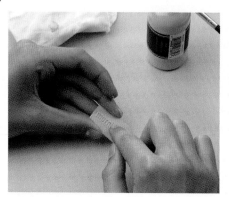

1 Select a metal word tag that has raised letters. Lightly sand the tag and clean it of oil and dust. Paint the raised letters your chosen color.

2 While the paint is still wet, lightly run your fingertip across the painted, raised letters and along the tag edges.

3 Holding the tag with tweezers, carefully dip it into melted extra thick embossing powder. Allow the tag to dry before lacing a ribbon through the hole.

Coldwater Creek Adventure Challenge

Once in a while a sporting experience just can't be photographed, but that doesn't mean that it can't be scrapbooked, as proven by this terrific page. No photos, but a plethora of papers, layered and inked, stamped and distressed, along with embellishments and journaling, tell the story beautifully.

Madeline Fox

Set Sail

Sailing is like flying on water, and this page captures the magic of that experience. Diamond shapes are layered and mounted on a serene cardstock background to create a unique platform for this serene sailboat photo. A prominent stamped title, handwritten journaling strips, brads, wispy ribbon and gentle half moon gem accents carry forward the peaceful scene.

Shimelle Laine

> *Oh, swiftly glides the bonnie boat, Just parted from the shore, And to the fisher's chorus-note, Soft moves the dipping oar!*
>
> *Joanna Baillie*

The River Wild

A wild white water adventure is captured with this graphic title block that serves double-duty as a photo mat. The title is printed, torn, inked, and mounted on light and dark stitched green cardstock. A tag and adventure definition embellish the page that sports photos reflecting the high energy fun of the experience.

Mary MacAskill

U Only Live Once

An earth tone palette allows the blues and reds in these photos to pop. Bits of canvas hug photo corners, providing texture for the title, and help the punched-out letter stencil to demand attention.

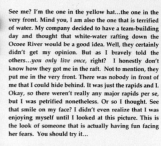

See me? I'm the one in the yellow hat...the one in the very front. Mind you, I am also the one that is terrified of water. My company decided to have a team-building day and thought that white-water rafting down the Ocoee River would be a good idea. Well, they certainly didn't get my opinion. But as I bravely told the others...*you only live once*, right? I honestly don't know how they got me in the raft. Not to mention, they put me in the very front. There was nobody in front of me that I could hide behind. It was just the rapids and I. Okay, so there weren't really any major rapids per se, but I was petrified nonetheless. Or so I thought. See that smile on my face? I didn't even realize that I was enjoying myself until I looked at this picture. This is the look of someone that is actually having fun facing her fears. You should try it...

WorldTravel Partners (ATL) team-building day
Ocoee River, TN - 1998

Camilla Bauman, Photo: Marcene Lynch

Rolling Down the Chatahoochie

This layout is packed with fun and photos. The strips of photos on the right side of the layout (below) don't leave out a single detail. Their horizontal placement aligns with the river current. Index tabs with journaling prompts make for fast, fun, and attention-getting photo captions as they help separate the images.

She Scores!

Including multiple photos on a layout allows you to tell even more of the story. Keep embellishments to a minimum, accenting photos with smaller, less obtrusive items such as photo turns, staples, or strips of paper.

Alecia Ackerman Grimm

Shelby Valadez

Go Go Go

Light blue and white cardstock rectangles are mounted on a darker cardstock background and overlaid with a printed transparency on this go-for-it page. A large photo and a smaller supporting photo are balanced by the bold, "go go, go" stamped title.

The Color Guy

Fish Factoids

People are talking about fish, oh boy, are they talking! And here are some of the things they think we should all know: (We can't say if they're true, but, hey, they're fun!)

It is illegal in Kansas to catch a fish with your bare hands.

The catfish has over 27,000 taste buds.

Male seahorses give birth to as many as 400 babies at a time.

If you keep a goldfish in a dark room it may actually turn white over time.

Starfish have no brain.

A shark is the only fish that can blink with both eyes.

A goldfish has a memory span of three seconds.

The giant squid has the largest eyes in the world.

A pregnant goldfish is called a "twit."

The largest fish ever caught was a whale shark and it was 59 feet long.

Fish can't live in the Dead Sea because it is too salty.

The largest pearl ever found in an oyster was 620 carats.

A shrimp's heart is in its head.

Lisa Schmitt

Big Air

Bold edge-to-edge vertical striped papers with a coordinating circle pattern draw your eye to the panoramic cropped photo on the left page of this superior layout. Sections of photo and transparency are divided and aligned to match precisely along the two inner page edges, adding to a sense of continuity and flow across the spread.

She Scores!

Attaching transparencies with snaps accomplishes two tasks, adding to the page design and simultaneously holding the transparencies in place.

Adventure

Abstract watercolor designs on saturated blue patterned paper are the perfect complement to pages about wet 'n' wild fun in this mini book filled with adventurous vacation pages. The artist balances photos with fun border elements, including a layered tag secured with ribbon, and embellished mesh that looks like fish netting.

Mary Jo Johnston

Swim Powered Sports

The deep blue—whether it's the bottom of a swimming pool, or a tropical bay, just calls for splashing humans. And we answer the summons with goggles, fins, scuba tanks, polo balls and other sports equipment that make it possible for us to leave behind earth and become one with the fish. Scrapbook your aquatic experiences on splashy scrapbook pages.

Andrea Deer

Swimming YMCA

Most swimmers begin learning the basics at an early age, and this young athlete is no exception. His efforts are celebrated with a palette of lime green and water blue. A clear sticker strip is swiped with green paint and tied with ribbons before being mounted between the two distinct photos. Accents, including brads, stickers, and blue cardstock circles add their own lively touch of fun.

H20 Polo

Water polo is aggressive, exhausting and utterly exhilarating, as seen on this clean and simple layout. Stark white cardstock provides a background for a series of dynamic photos, an intricately-cut cardstock title, and a text block.

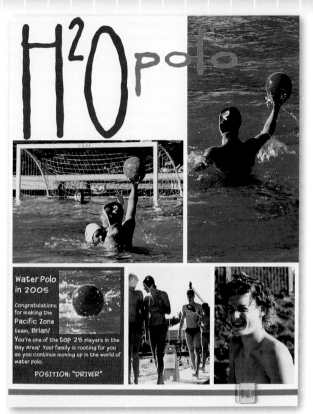

Kathleen Summers

> **❝** *I didn't know one thing about the sport. I used to wonder how they got the horses in the pool.* **❞**
>
> *Dick Enberg*

Love 2 Scuba Dive

The curving lines within the pattern of a beautiful piece of paper provide cutting guidelines for carving out the flowing paper block seen on this page. The cut shape is mounted over the lower photo and then to a coordinating patterned paper background. A frenzy of letters, including letter magnets, tags, epoxy letters, and rub-ons, create the title. A pull-out journaling card slips under the top photo.

Paula Barber

Susan Weinroth

Trunk Bay

Perfectly matched blue and green card-stocks and patterned papers pull colors from both sea and sky on this snorkeling page. Heartfelt journaling, printed on vellum, describes a bay that is almost too beautiful to be real. Important words are bolded and highlighted to bring interest to the journaled border.

Mexico

Snorkeling can be fun and relaxing, especially in foreign waters. The colors on this lovely page capture the experience with splashes of ocean-blue water and sandy earth tones. Small portions of patterned papers along two corners, fabric letters and printed twill add a rich texture. The title and large "explore" journaling blocks balance each other. The offset matted photo is stapled to the page, leaving a pocket behind for a journaled tag.

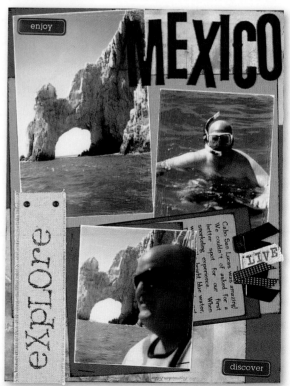

Katina Matheson

Sand, Waves, Sun

There is nothing like a beach and a boogie board to make an ocean adventure complete. The photos on this page are adhered to the cardstock background and overlaid with printed transparencies. A stunning border, made with tiny sea shells, sea glass, and a small bottle, decorates the bottom of the page.

Jackie Siperko

Create a decorative shell border

1 Use a brush to spread Paper Perfect (a paint product that creates the look of paper) over a strip of mesh. Apply the paint thicker in some areas and less thick in others. Allow the paint to dry.

2 Ink the mesh before adhering shells with a strong craft glue. Allow the decorated mesh to dry, then mount it to your scrapbook page.

3 Journal on a piece of vellum. Cut another piece of vellum in the shape of a bottle. Embellish the vellum bottle before slipping both it and the journaling beneath the mounted mesh.

Creating Humorous Sports Scrapbook Pages

Yes, sports are about competition, but they are also all about FUN—a concept that can be hard to remember in this "let's win!" world. So keeping your eye on the true rewards of athletic involvement is important. Why not create scrapbook sports pages that remind you that athletics, like scrapbooking, should be a romp of laughter, friendship, and growth? Capture those just-plain-silly sporting moments in your scrapbook art, or push the envelope and dream up some out-there sports that don't (and maybe should?) exist? Your pages will be trophies of truly memorable sporting moments.

Kris Gillespie

3...18...40...

A story of a long and very creative day of ball activity is displayed on this scrapbook spread. Photos are mounted in what appears to be random placement on a white cardstock background, providing a childlike mood. Stitching, drawn directly on the black bottom border photo mat, carries the "let's play ball" theme.

Extreme Jet Ski Football

It looks almost too realistic to be digital, and yet that that's exactly how this page was made. Digital papers, tags, water droplets, and even stitching and brads were created with a computer. The action photos hold their own against the vibrant palette, and the journaling adds a creative and humorous voice.

Give a boy a football, motorized toy and free time and a new extreme sport is born.

Angie Svoboda

Sledding in the Snow

This wild and crazy page, introducing a new action sport concept, was created digitally, including patterned papers, brads, snowflakes, and the title. The bright colors in the photos help them pop on this monochromatic winter palette.

Angie Svoboda

From the Color Guy

Little Known Sports (believe it or not, we are not making these up) that Really DO Exist

Buzkashi: Played in Afghanistan, mounted players try to snatch a carcass of a goat or calf (often headless) from the middle of a playing field and carry it across a goal line.

Jai-Alai: An ancient Basque or Spanish game played in a court with a ball and a wickerwork racket. Its name means, "merry festival" in Basque. This game holds the distinction of involving the fastest moving ball in any ball game, with the object flying at approximately 170 miles an hour.

Elephant Polo: Governed by The World Elephant Polo Association, which was founded in 1982, this game is played in Nepal on an airstrip. The rules are similar to those followed by pony-riding polo players.

Mountain Unicycling: This perilous recreational sport attracts dyed-in-the-wool unicyclists who thrill at the idea of riding their one-wheeled bikes over rough terrain. These same athletes may also play unicycle hockey (another little known sport).

Toe Wrestling: A sport started in England in 1976 in which shoeless competitors lock toes. When the ump yells, "Toes away!" the competitors try to push down the toes of their opponent, very much as in arm wrestling.

Camel Wrestling: A popular sport in Turkey, the specially bred camels are dressed in colorful uniforms and are led into a ring where they go at it. Fans place bets as the animals attempt to better their opponent.

Butt Boarding: This racing sport is performed on a non-motorized vehicle resembling a large skateboard. Competitors, both professional and amateur, race for prizes down steep and often snaking paved courses.

Wife Carrying: The competition, which draws athletes from around the world, takes place in Finland. Male contestants sling their wives over their shoulders and carry them around an obstacle-strewn course. Drop the Little Woman, and you receive a time penalty and may end up sleeping on the couch. The winner is awarded his wife's weight in beer.

Caber Toss: A popular sport in the Scottish Highland Games, this competition requires the athlete to balance a large wooden pole in his arms, run forward and toss the pole. The winner is the athlete who scores the longest toss.

Ice Skating

Some like it cold. Brrrrr. Ice and snow sports provide many with shivery fun and exercise. Sports that call for a pair of boots with sharp silver blades also call for incredible balance and fluidity. Ice hockey, a sport that has grown in popularity across America in recent years, pushes athletes to the wall and back, demanding skill, speed and strength. Scrapbook this sport for slick pages.

Wendy Gibson

Hockey Player

The puck is gonna take a beating, if this photo is indicative of the action that followed. The image is further strengthened by the printed transparency overlaying its lower portion. The transparency slips onto the background cardstock and papers as well. Ribbon-tied tags are tacked down with photo turns. When released, they can be turned over to reveal journaling. Buttons and sticker details are added to the finished page.

Game Day

A series of large photos set on a palette of black and red card-stocks is supported by a creative strip title treatment An upper page border made with stickers, laces, and journaled hockey term blocks helps balance the powerful distressed photos below.

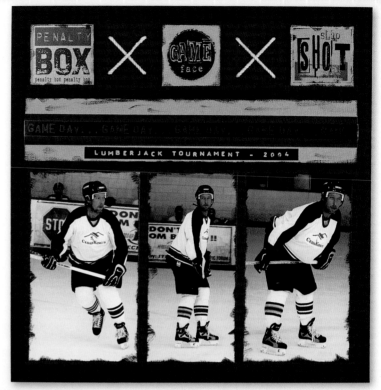

Wendy Gibson

Renae Clark

Badger State Games

Dry-brushed white painted blocks of red, blue, and white patterned paper are layered over black cardstock on this slick spread. The brush marks convey a sense of motion. A photo of the awarded medal, winner's race results, and a tribute letter are displayed on tags.

Lori Ann Frey

Anticipation

Rub-ons on top of hockey tape create a unique title for this page, that is heavy with ingenuity. Overlapping elements of layered cardstock, patterned paper, stickers, and definitions surround the large focal photo. A collection of tags holds extra images and journaling.

She Scores!

A collection of tags are tied together with a real hockey skate lace, giving this page a shot of authenticity.

String together a tag booklet using spare images

1 Use a template to draw tag shapes on pieces of cardstock. Cut out the shapes before setting eyelets in each tag.

2 Decorate the tags with stickers, decorative paper and sections of spare photos.

3 String a hockey lace or ribbon through the tag eyelets and add charms before mounting the tag booklet to your scrapbook page.

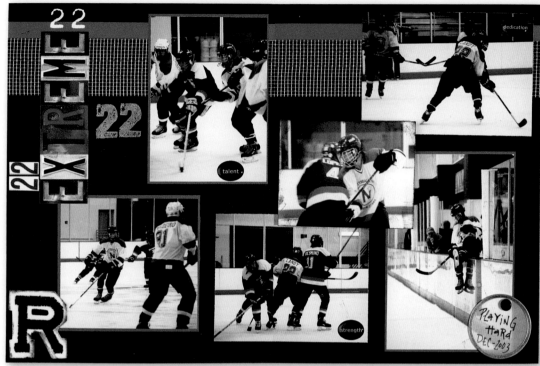

Allison Landy

Extreme

With a quick shutter finger, this artist captures action-packed hockey photos. The focal photo is mounted with foam adhesive that pops the photo up from the background paper, drawing the viewer's eye. A band of mesh and a photo stride across the page seam, creating a visually cohesive spread.

All Stars

The American spirit of athletic competitiveness is captured on this red, white, and blue layout. Inked and layered cardstocks and black printed paper convey the roughness of the game. A beaded chain anchors handwritten accounts of the season, and is bound with eyelets and jump rings.

Allison Landy

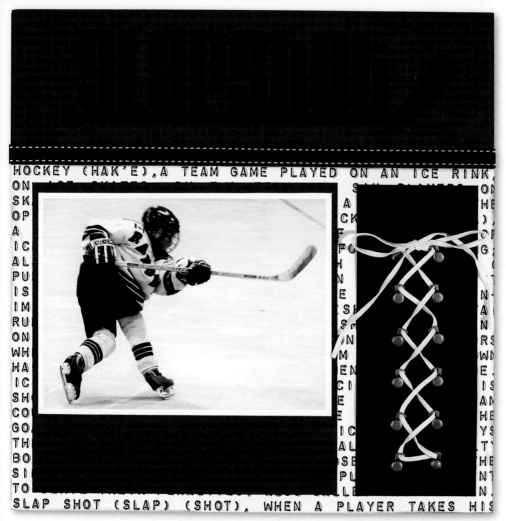

Slapshot

An action photo, mounted on a red textured journaling block and placed on a patterned paper background, takes center ice on this hockey page. The bold black title treatment is mounted on a block of red cardstock. A stitched black ribbon overlays the seam between cardstock and patterned paper. Brads, laced and mounted on a black paper block, add embellishment while mimicking a hockey skate.

Kim Jones

Make a boldly laced page border

1 Use a light colored pencil to make perpendicular marks along a strip of dark cardstock. Use a punch to create holes in cardstock.

2 Set looped brads in each of the holes in the cardstock.

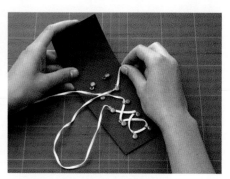

3 Use a crisscross pattern to string a shoelace through the brad loops before tying the lace in a bow.

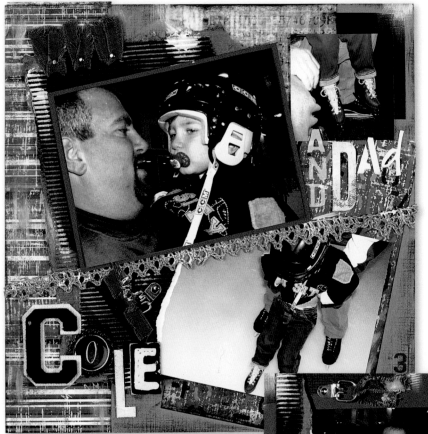

No Gretzky

Rich with texture, this spread draws its charm from a collage of paint, ink, stickers, rub-ons, decorative brads, and other three dimensional elements. Enlarged photos show off the young skater and journaling hidden behind a photo tells the story of a busy day of instruction and activity.

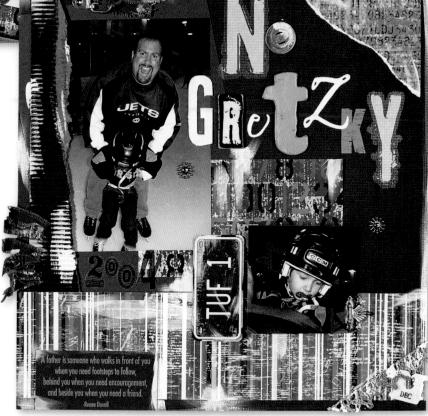

> **" I don't like my hockey sticks touching other sticks, and I don't like them crossing one another, and I kind of have them hidden in the corner. I put baby powder on the ends. I think it's essentially a matter of taking care of what takes care of you. "**
>
> *Wayne Gretzky*

Mikki Livanos

Snow Sports

Skiing, tubing, snowmobiling and other sports are reasons to play in that wonderful fluffy white stuff—snow! Who can resist? Snow sport pages can be built with cool blues that convey a feeling of wintery weather, or utilize hot colors such as reds, pinks and yellows that convey a sense of bundled-up fun. Scrapbook these snowy good times and remember them long after the last snowflake has melted.

Ticee Moore

Rough Ride

Gray, cool purples and blues are a perfect palette choice for this super cool winter sports page. A striking snowlike embossed title and tags tied with ribbon support the many photos of winter fun.

Fun

What could be more fun that a day on a sledding hill? This colorful page captures the chill with cool blue and green textured cardstocks, and captures the thrill with layered colorful patterned papers. A large "S" stencil screams "snow," the theme of the day. Colorful brads, buttons, ribbons and safety pins contribute zing to the layout.

Angela Moen

Snow Day

Does this young athlete have a future on a luge team? That remains to be seen, but one thing is clear, this page captures the fun of a favorite winter sport. A large white title over cool purple cardstock and coordinating patterned papers captures the chilly weather feeling of the day. Sparkling snowflake embellishments, acrylic words and ribbons, along with a series of supporting photos complete the page.

> **"** *What fire could ever equal the sunshine of a winter's day?* **"**
>
> *Henry David Thoreau*

Andrea Deer

Angela Biggley

Wipe Out

It's the contrast between brilliant yellow and gray that makes this page something to celebrate. The model's jacket and sled, as well as the yellow labels, are set against a gray cardstock background and definition paper. The chipboard letters used to create the title are painted, while the journaling block below is printed on a transparency.

Too Cool

This page proves that juicy colors can be trendy in any season. The hot pinks and warm reds spice up the page, while the cool blues and icy, industrial feeling of the letter stickers allude to the freezing temperatures. The blue pocket conceals journaling that memorializes the model's first tubing adventure.

She Scores!

For a clever spin and a fun reading experience document a day as though you were a weather forecaster.

Sherry Wright

Snow Baby

A hot pink inner tube sets the mood for this wintery page, which calls upon a palette of colors that are not traditionally associated with a wintery theme. The combination of patterned papers supports a vellum journaling block that is bordered with shimmery beads. Beaded snowflakes and metal snowflake charms turn up the chill factor. A ribbon-tied tag with an inked title complete the scene.

Sherry Wright

Angela Moen

Sledding

Layers of patterned papers perfectly support these photos of layered and bundled up children out for frosty-day sports fun. A strip of ribbon, an acrylic title, and embellished stencils wrap things up.

Snowboard!

White flowers with blue snowflake eyelets are an unconventional embellishment for this snow page. The design is built along a sloping diagonal that creates a sense of movement, following the snow bunny model as she careens down the hill. The ribbon accents look as if they are caught up in the action. Tags, Dymo labels, and a integrated title complete the layout.

She Scores!

Oversized flower embellishments work perfectly when placed in the opposite corner from the page title, giving the layout a balanced appeal.

Martine Giguère

There's nothing normal and everything extreme about it:
you ski like a maniac!

Whistler is no match for your
Double-Diamond-Daredevil SKILLS

Daredevil

EVEL KNIEVEL
AFRAID
DANGEROUS
MOTORCYCLE
STUNT

thomas

whistler
AIR

Tia Bennett

Skiing Daredevil

Winter-themed patterned papers set the icy tone for this thrill-seeking page. Photos and paper elements are carefully stitched for extra appeal. White rub-ons are applied over the blue sky in the photos. The edges of an acrylic block are painted white and mounted over a supporting photo with screw snaps for an appealing three-dimensional embellishment.

Snowmobiling

Photos so chilly that they have a bluish tint are set against blue and white background papers on this terrific page. A bold striped paper acts as a large photo mat for all the images. The snowmobiling definition and a date provide all the journaling necessary.

snowmobiling:

thomas

and the boys

A perfect combination of violent action
taking place in an atmosphere of total tranquility.

-BJ King

january
2005

Tia Bennett

You sold your motorcycle,
You messed up your knees skiing.
Now what?
Shredding up the mountain
At Snoqualmie,
It isn't hard to see why
You made the move
To snowmobiles.
Faster speed, rugged terrain,
And wicked cool versatility.

Play hard, showoff.

SNOWMOBILE

thomas   2005

play

Tia Bennett

She Scores!
Mounting copies of the same photo side by side creates a sense of motion, appropriate for this speedy page.

Snowmobile

There is no question at all about the theme of this wintery page—snowmobiling! A non-traditional color scheme of greens and reds make this layout pop. A playful stamped title looks as though it was created with packed snow, and the torn and layered journaling block provides information about the exciting day.

Creating Faux Sports Magazine Covers and Ads

Inspiration is everywhere including the magazine racks at your favorite store. If you find yourself running on empty creatively, pick up a few of your favorite sports magazines. The cover may provide just the inspiration you need to create your own sports magazine scrapbooking page. Or flip through the ads inside to find terrific ideas for page designs, color combinations, and techniques.

Kathleen Broadhurst

Baseball Digest

If he isn't a cover kid yet, he should be soon—as evidenced by this effective layout featuring a have-ball-will-play athlete. The clean title and journaling are printed on transparencies and then mounted. Shiny gold sports charms add a bit of gleam, and the red floss from which they dangle plays up the red photo mat.

She Scores!

The "All Boy" patterned paper is set on top of a piece of wire screen and sanded before being mounted. This gives it a rough-and-tumble look that matches the page concept.

Hockey Chick

This page looks like the cover of a sports magazine but is actually built on hockey-themed patterned paper. The focal photo is matted on cardstock, mesh, and patterned papers and mounted with shiny brads. The bold title is matted, inked and embellished with brads. Journaling is hidden under the primary photo and on twill tape mounted with eyelets.

She Scores!

The printed twill tape journaling strips are created by typing words on paper and printing. Then attach strips of twill tape above the printed words with double-sided tape. Run the paper through the printer again.

Nicole White

The Harder You Play

This dramatic page could take its place in any magazine as an advertisement for sports gear. Created digitally, it includes a screened-back action background, bold colors and drop-in thumbnail photos. The graphic result is a page that screams with energy.

Christie Acciarri-Smith

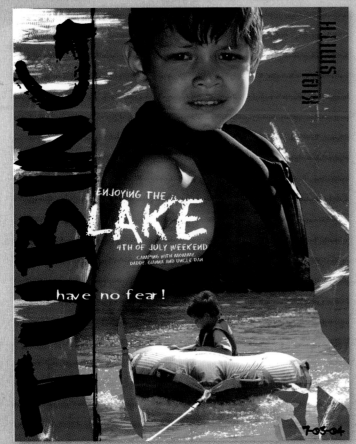

Christie Acciarri-Smith

Have No Fear

It could be an advertisement for an outdoor adventure company, but this scrapbook page actually recounts a day at the lake and the young tuber who faces down his fear. The excellent digitally-created scrapbook page beautifully incorporates both color and black-and-white photos as well as an aggressive font choice in its graphic design.

Max and Meagan

Just a spot of color picks up the pink in the model's head gear to give even more impact to a stunning focal photo. The rest of the colors play second fiddle with their earth tones, but their graphic patterns are anything but drab. The double-layered monograms add style and subtle color.

She Scores!
Delicate zigzag stitches in white add subtle texture and help unify the design by connecting all of the layers and patterns.

Laura McKinley

Ski Durango

Black-and-white photos illustrate a moment-by-moment skiing "whoops" on this ski-'til-you-drop page. The sequence of photos are journaled with concise labels. Patterned paper, silk flowers, and a mixed media title work to warm up the page in a whimsical fashion.

Missy Neal

Winter

Placing the photo on its side shows the serious vertical slope this skier successfully navigated. The torn and tattered office manila envelope shouts the theme of repeated ski successes and leaves plenty of lines for one-word descriptive journaling.

She Scores!
Crumpled blue tissue paper enhanced with white acrylic paint gives the appearance of frosty, icy snow. Wipes of blue acrylic paint on the envelope keep the layout's temperature low.

Laura McKinley

Create an eye-catching tissue background

1 Crumple a piece of blue tissue paper. Open the tissue once again and gently smooth out some of the wrinkles.

2 Adhere the top and bottom edges of the crumpled and smoothed tissue to your cardstock background using a decoupage medium.

3 Ink or paint the raised ridges of the tissue to add visual dimension. Allow the tissue to dry before mounting your photo.

Sherri Wright

Chapter Three
Personal Best

A good quote for my next
scrapbook page.

"Horses and children, I often think,
have a lot of the good sense there
is in the world."

~Josephine DeMott Robinson

Equestrian Sports

Ask most any child what she wants for her birthday, and the answer is likely to be, "a pony!" The joy of riding is hard to beat, and the type of steed and saddle seem to have very little to do with the pleasure of feeling the wind in your face and hearing hoofbeats beneath you. Scrapbook equestrian sports on rustic pages that capture that special connection between animals and humans.

Kitty Foster, Photos: Linda Lee Keeble

She Scores!
Don't let the earth tones and rugged textures fool you—this page is a subtle testament to girl power. To infuse the right amount of femininity, the photos are matted with a purple symbolic of womanly strength.

Sweetheart of the Rodeo

A mix of assorted patterned papers are layered to form the background for this rodeo page which draws its strength from the variety of angles captured in the photos. A creative title flows from the upper left hand page corner to the lower right, utilizing a variety of supplies to make its statement, including definition stickers and twill letters. Silver conchos and a heart clip, nicely round up this rodeo layout.

Corry Heinricks

Learning to Ride

This photo represents the sole salvage-able image of a series the artist took to document the model's riding class, so she enlarged it for impact. The eye-catching blue mat was inspired by the model's shirt. To keep the page rustic, the back-ground is layered with inked and torn brown papers. The striped ribbon ties everything together.

She Scores!

For quick customized metal-rimmed tags, print the desired captions onto patterned paper. Punch out the captions to match the size of the tag. Adhere the punched shapes to the tag, leaving just enough metal showing for glimmer and gleam.

Pony Ride

The tiny cowgirl in this photo can concen-trate on developing her riding skills while others enjoy this rustic page. Layered blocks of coordinating patterned papers create an illusion of depth, while pro-viding a background for the compelling photo. The edges of most elements are either sanded or inked. The title includes stamped letters and sanded and painted chipboard letters. Journaling, ribbons and buckles, as well as a colorful floral embel-lishment, complete the scene.

She Scores!

Anchor an asymmetrical layout with a simple yet eye-catching corner embellishment. The overlapping and embellished ribbon and flower accent balances the heavy title. The orange flower adds needed color to offset the earth tones.

Laura Ward

Best in Show

One way to add an artistic and unique effect to a page is to digitally enhance a photo with a texture filter. Simply import a photo into an image-editing program, create a duplicate image in which to work, and experiment with the options under the filter menu. Here, the artist creates a watercolor rendering for the horse photo.

Laura McKinley

Create a decorative buckle

1 Cut strips of paper to your desired width. Bend one end of each strip through a buckle opening. Set an eyelet to close the paper strip and prevent the buckle from slipping free.

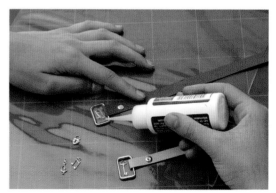

2 Place the buckle on a nonstick work surface. Set a charm in the center of the buckle form. Fill the center of the buckle form with clear gloss. Allow the gloss to dry before mounting it on your page.

Fly

This layout is symbolic of the enduring struggles athletes and their animal counterparts must overcome to reach such a high competitive level. The photos are so powerful they almost fly off the page. Patterned paper, letter stickers and metal tags work perfectly with the journaling blocks.

She Scores!

Successfully photographing athletes in motion is tricky, so set up your camera where dramatic action is most likely to take place. Focus your camera and wait. Try to anticipate the action before it arrives, so you'll be able to take the photo instantaneously.

Concerto and Leslie Howard

*Harmony, power, grace and courage
—a perfect partnership.
Two athletes working in concert,
each believing in the other,
striving to conquer immense obstacles
standing between them and
victory.
Their performance culminates
years of hard work, dedication and
determination.
The Olympic dream
is always just a fraction of an inch
away.*

*Festival Of Champions
Gladstone, New Jersey*

> **Of all creatures God made at the Creation, there is none more excellent or so much to be respected, as a horse.**
>
> *Legend*

Tricia Booker

Kathleen Broadhurst, Photos: Theresa Bertrand

Alexis & Tia

The strong red of the model's vest would make it tempting to use red as a secondary accent color. But, the artist rightfully resisted, using red only to lightly accent the title. The result is photos that pop off a background created with a successful mix of patterned papers. The gingham ribbon adds a nice pattern contrast and connects all of the page elements.

The Color Guy
Famous Horses

Athletes assume star status throughout the world, and it is no different with equestrian sports. However the renowned athletes in this arena are more likely to have four legs than two. In fact, horses have been considered celebrities throughout the ages. Here are some of history's most recognized horse heroes.

Pegasus: a winged horse from Greek lore. Pegasus was ridden by Bellerophon, and they had glorious adventures together. Those good times came to an end when Bellerophon attempted to ride Pegasus over Mt. Olympus. He was thrown to Earth, and Pegasus flew off, never to be seen again.

Bucephalus: tamed and ridden by Alexander the Great. Bucephalus carried Alexander into many battles before dying himself of battle wounds in 326 B.C. Alexander is said to have been distraught over his horse's death and built a city to commemorate the heroic steed.

Comanche: survived Custer's Last Stand. Comanche is said to have been owned by an officer who fought with Custer in his battle against Chief Sitting Bull, Crazy Horse and their warriors. Comanche is said to have been the only survivor from Custer's ranks.

Man o' War: considered by many to be the best race horse of all time. Man o' War won twenty out of twenty-one races in which he ran. He died and was embalmed in 1947.

Maria Gallardo-Williams

Sports Do not Build Character...

This vibrant spread is all about patterned paper and a mix of shapes. The large circle elements layered over striped patterned paper is a symbolic graphic representation of the ribbons won by the model and her equestrian companion. By choosing a color palette a bit more muted than that found in the photos, the artist creates a background full of pizzazz while keeping the focus on the photos.

Team of Two

A simple, well-executed design is the hallmark of this layout. Horizontal striped patterned paper, minimal journaling, a strong title and vertical photos are carefully placed for proportion. The nibble of lilac in the paper helps pop the photo as it relates to the model's shirt.

Kathy Thompson Laffoley

Sports on a Roll

It's a mystery who designed the first wheel, but it is believe he lived in Asia around 8,000 B.C. That first crude wheel was most likely just a rolling wooden log upon which a heavy object was placed and pushed forward. Today's wheels are a far cry from those ancient devices. High tech, they spin at incredible speeds, taking athletes across the miles and across countless finish lines. Scrapbook these fast-paced sports on racy, exciting pages.

Laura Stewart

What Goes Up, Must Come Down

Mountain biking is not for the faint of heart, but photos of the challenging sport can make exciting scrapbook pages. A sanded paper background overlaid with strips of paper and a matted photo dominate this page. Journaling is on the back. A rustic tag, decorated with a bike charm, tile, floss, beads, brads and twine embellish the layout.

Ride

Distressed paper blocks support powerful dirt bike images on this rough-and-tough page. Closely cropped photos of both the rider and his ride are displayed under a large metallic filmstrip frame on the left page. A panoramic picture of the same rider has been digitally cropped into seven sections and then mounted across the bottom of the right page. Buttons, ribbon, a label, shiny brads, and journaling, complete this blue-ribbon spread.

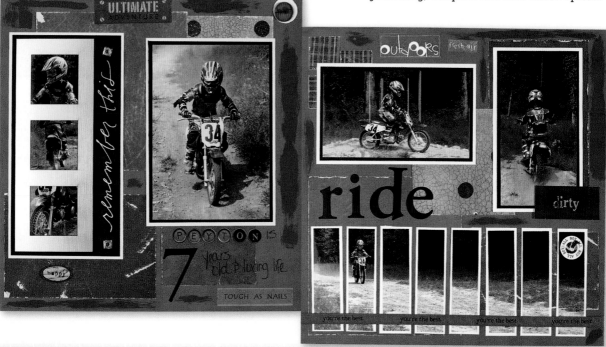

LeAnn Fane

We Bike

Everything about this page is wedded in thematic bliss. The background paper is made with texture paint, ink and a real bike tire. The distressed font continues the rugged, muddied feel of the page, and the shiny duct tape used to attach the journaling block echoes the sheen of the model's bike helmet.

We **BIKE** to feel our blood pumping and our lungs burn. We bike to feel the sun on our backs and the **MUD** on our faces. We bike to awaken our sense of **ADVENTURE**

Derrick, Mary, Justyna & Devin
Elbow Falls, Spring 2004

Mary MacAskill, Photo: Derrick MacAskill

Create a muddy textured background

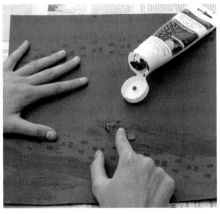

1 Spread newspapers across your work surface. Ink a bike tire heavily. Roll the tire across a sheet of brown cardstock. Allow the inked paper to dry thoroughly.

2 Use your finger or an applicator to apply texture paste to the inked cardstock. Allow the paste to dry.

3 Ink the ruts to create the illusion of even more dimension.

Speed Racer

This page cranks up heart rates with vibrant red cardstock and layered black and white paper elements. An index-folder flip book calls attention to the focal photo and also houses the support photos. The cleverly numbered tabs invite a reader to view the book sequentially and be enticed by the announcer-style journaling that accompanies each photo.

Dana Tuskey

She Scores!

Scrapbooking and sports are fun. Bring a sense of lightheartedness to your pages through humor. This artist shows her quirky side by describing the photo sequence as if the drivers were racing enthusiasts only to reveal they were the sole drivers on the track that day.

Fast Ride

To keep in motion with the racing subject matter of the photo, a checkered paper is aggressively sanded and smudged with ink, then placed on black cardstock. A monogrammed tag, customized with inked tire tracks from a child's toy car, is stapled for a rugged look and accompanied by a metal mesh border strung along the bottom. The "Fast Ride" title shouts out the page theme.

Christina Husk

Dirt Bike

Vibrant red papers charge this dirt biking page with high energy. All elements on the page, including the shiny brads, are digitally created. Even the layered title seems to be aggressive, appearing to pop right off the page.

Sherry Cartwright

One of the highlights of visiting my family in Ohio is getting to watch Nana and Papa race! Kiersten thinks it is pretty cool to get to go to the racetrack and watch all the fast cars race down the track. And to see her Nana win trophies! It gets pretty loud there with all the racing engines but nothing a good pair of earphones can't solve! There aren't too many grandchildren that can say they get to watch their Nana and Papa race cars and Kiersten thinks that is pretty cool!

Racing

Fast Cars

Fun!

Heather Preckel

She Scores!
The focus of this page is the truck wheels, and that circular shape is repeated again and again for a dramatic effect. Polka dot patterned paper, a circular journaling block, three bulleted circles, a circle embellished border strip and rounded photo edges and corners carry on the theme.

Drag Racing
Sharply focused photographs are the main attraction on this layout, capturing and reinforcing rounded structures throughout evenly spaced circles and corners. A strip of polka dots draws the eye down toward a simple black cardstock background, while a contrasting white inked border and journaling details set the racing mood in motion.

BMX

Layered blocks of rustic patterned papers make this page a feast of visual variety. The photos are matted with additional patterned papers. A concise, matted title block provides an island of calm on the high-energy page. Letter and number stickers finish up the layout.

> *It is only when you are pursued that you become swift.*
>
> *Kahlil Gibran*

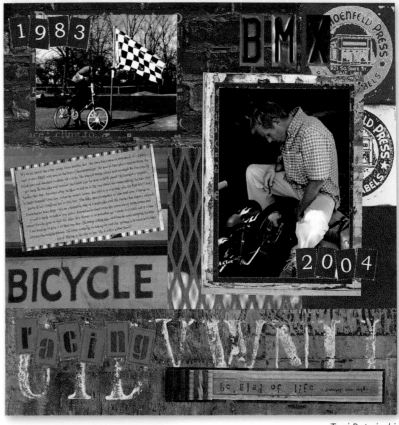

Tarri Botwinski

X-Treme Sport Race

Winning that first gold medal is an important event in every athlete's life, and this x-tremely good page showcases that win. A handmade stencil, and distressed elements provide the page with a very masculine feeling. Knotted gingham ribbon honors the checkered-flag motif found in the model's racing gear. The industrial-strength title speaks loudly enough to be heard over an engine's roar.

Johanna Peterson

Scrapbooking Sports Memorabilia
Let's face it, "Stuff" is cool. And collecting sports-related stuff like ticket stubs and newspaper clippings, autographed photos of sports heros, badges and programs is part of the fun of being an athlete or fan. Don't forget to include those neat mementoes on your scrapbook pages. Like your photos, these items will be cherished throughout the years.

Dawn Burden

26.2 Miles
Bring color and interest to a scrapbook page while preserving a race day number. Attach the number to the page with safety pins for an additional touch of authenticity. Showcase photos of the young runner wearing the number on both sides of the spread.

At the Salle
Why rely strictly on photos to recall a sporting activity when you can include a DVD of the events? This very graphic, color-blocked page is inspired by the block-patterned paper. The flowing script portions of both the journaling and title work to soften the look of the design.

She Scores!
Include a DVD of a sporting event, or tuck a disc of additional photo images on a page for safe storage.

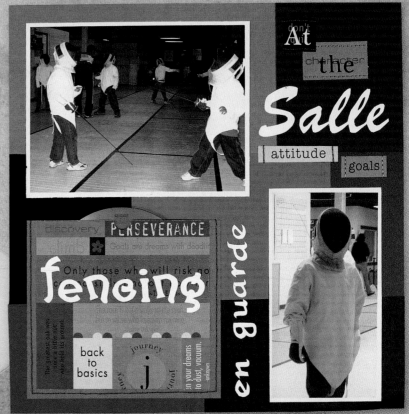

Tarri Botwinski

The Perfect Game

Nary a strike exists on this spread, which is full of interactive elements that engage the reader in the story. Several memorabilia pockets house newspaper clippings, the tickets and a tag series with extensive journaling. A brochure, tucked into homemade photo corners, keeps the information-packed parcel secure, yet accessible to curious readers.

Lonni McMullen

She Scores!

When taking winning photos at a professional sporting event is almost impossible, use a brochure as your page's focal point. Support the primary image with shots of your own and with memorabilia.

Jarome Iginia Rocks!

A photo of a sports hero is a terrific piece of memorabilia. Photograph both the memorabilia and its owner for a awesome scrapbook page. Textured red cardstock, mounted on a black background, supports the photo. Concise journaling and a tiny ice skate sticker are all that are needed to bring this page home.

Kerry Zerff

People Powered Sports

Legs were meant for running and rolling, arms for pushing and pulling, and there are slews of popular sports that call upon human muscles for motivation and motorization. Track and field, weight lifting, roller skating and blading, golf and other individual sports are fueled by human energy alone. It is all about digging deep and finding core strength to drive the body and the mind to meet a goal. Scrapbook these individual events that pit man against himself, a clock, or perhaps even a tiny hole at the far end of an expanse of grass.

Gemiel Matthews

Anticipation

Not one bit of action is left for the reader to deduce, because the photos on this page show everything from the relay hand-off to the determined sprint. An offset focal-photo frame adds energy and points the reader to the journaling block. The bold snippets of text in the journaling block draw the eye.

The Color Guy
Taking Great Sports Photos

Getting just the right action-packed sports photo can be as challenging as hitting a long ball over a sand trap. Experts offer these suggestions:

- Take photos during practices rather than games. You may be able to move closer to the field in order to snap close-ups. And, as practices generally involve lots of drills and repetition, you have more than one chance to follow and capture the action.

- Try to sit on the same side as your favorite player so you won't have to shoot over the heads of other athletes.

- Anticipate the action. Focus your camera on one likely spot and wait until your athlete enters your view.

- Use fast film (minimum of 200 ISO) to cut down on blurriness, and forget the flash when shooting large playing fields.

- Try to shoot early morning or late afternoon games and matches in order to minimize shadows.

- Don't limit your shots to your own special athlete. Take photos of the fans, the referees, and the field. These "extra" shots will give your other shots perspective when you scrapbook.

- Shoot close-ups of skinned knees, sweaty brows and flying hair as well as those full-body shots.

- Do NOT yell, "Honey, smile for the camera!" or any such thing, or you may find yourself yellow-carded by the family member you are trying to photograph!

Allison Landy

She Scores!

Create your own unique metal title block by embossing your selected word on a soft piece of metal. Ink the raised letters to give them more definition. Stamp the supporting word on the metal strip and embellish it with a distressed red metal frame.

Brute Strength

This incredibly strong layout supports its theme beautifully with a color-blocked background of black, gray and red cardstocks covered with heavy duty mesh. A vellum journaling block is inked before being set inside a severed and painted metal frame.

Run Fast Hard

Capturing images of sporting events is difficult. Common obstacles include distance, distracting backgrounds, and a moving target. Overcome such challenges by capturing a winning focal photo. Use less spectacular shots as supporting images, as seen on this page. The bold title frames the photos and a matted journaling block grounds the layout.

Missy Crowell

Let the Good Times Roll

For kids, skateboarding represents both fun and freedom, and this page captures the sport at its best. Layered cardstock and patterned papers work with a multimedia title that includes stickers, acrylic and tile letters. A filmstrip, slipped behind the focal photo, is tied with fibers, and buttons and holds down the lower right corner of the page.

Carol Darilek

Our "X" Games

Urban grittiness is captured on this spread, built on slabs of cardboard. More than a dozen photos are inked and mounted to the pages, which are embellished with mesh, clips, screw heads and staples. Handwritten journaling and Dymo labels add minimal, but important, information.

Carlene Federer

Sk8r Boy

Skater boys are cool and deserve only the coolest of titles. The messy appearance of the stamped title letters appear urban and hip, a look that is enhanced by the metal plaques that the letters are stamped upon. The orange complementary color is lifted from the smallest orange buckle found in the focal photos.

She Scores!
Look to the photos for accent ideas. The ribbon echoes the straps of the knee pads; the eyelets echo wheels; the paper echoes the grittiness of cement.

Kerry Zerff

Ready for Landing

The intersecting stripes of the patterned paper are perfect metaphors for movement on this layout. They also help direct the eye to the photos. Masculine detail is achieved with metallic mesh paper, metal accents and bits of distressing. The small journaling folder is painted to match the metallic feel of the page.

She Scores!
Use slide mounts to zoom in on page details. The pint-sized framing elements allow the artist to focus on two things intrinsically connected to the page—the helmet and knee pads— necessities in order for the model to be "ready for landing."

Kim Toomay

Karate Orange Belt

Belt testing is an important day in the life of every karate student and this page perfectly illustrates the pride of achievement. Black cardstock with a distressed appearance is overlaid with torn and inked patterned paper. Journaling blocks include Asian symbols and sayings. Small metal frames and a substantial "believe in yourself" fiber-tied plaque add kick.

Terri Bradford

> **The ultimate aim of Karate lies not in victory or defeat, but in the perfection of the character of its participants.**
>
> *Master Gichin Funakoshi*

Michelle McGowan

Believe in Yourself

A flood of red cardstock sets the powerful mood for this karate spread. Yellow photo mats, journaling strips and a stamped dragon add a blaze of accent color. Emotional journaling on the right page includes an original poem. Embellishments include metal tags, a ball chain, brads, stickers and eyelets.

Extreme

A series of both posed and action photos capture all the details of this adrenaline-packed story. A battered and crumpled paint chip supports the theme of the layout (left). The knotted strips of canvas fabric echo the frayed feelings of a loving mother who comes to terms with her son's love for an extreme sport. A tag, brads, and journaling strips embellish the layout.

She Scores!

The distinct journaling block is printed on a sepia print of a photo of the model. The photo is inked, rolled and torn to work with the rugged theme of the extreme sport.

Dawn Burden

Sue Fields, Team Photo: Jennifer Jones, Fredericks Photography

Golf

A fun harlequin print conjures up images of argyle-clad golfers strolling the links on this up-to-par spread. The linear pattern of the paper, with daggers of color used to mat the group photo, is reminiscent of golf tees. The, metallic accents and distressed feel lend a masculine edge to the page. A large memorabilia pocket holds a plethora of newspaper clippings that recount successes and losses of the young athlete.

She Scores!

High school sports accomplishments can be savored for years if they are stored in a memorabilia pocket. Arrange newspaper clippings so they extend from the pocket, becoming an intrinsic part of the page design. Decorate the pocket with a team photo.

A Good Walk Spoiled

Golf-patterned paper is a befitting background to showcase this sporty portrait. The off-kilter mat contrasts with the linear lines found within the tone-on-tone patterned paper. A strip of ribbon placed on the diagonal breaks up the page and helps anchor the photo. A title tag featuring a famous old golf quote and tiny journaled strips score this page a hole in one.

Sue Fields

score

Score

A collection of fun tags, ribbon and stitching carries the mood for this tennis page. A simple title and an action packed photo are all that's needed to complete the playful scene.

love

to

05

Laura McKinley

Create a personalized decorative tag embellishment

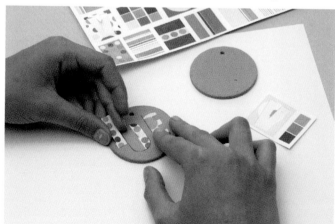

1 Apply colorful sticker letters to a wooden tag to spell out your chosen message.

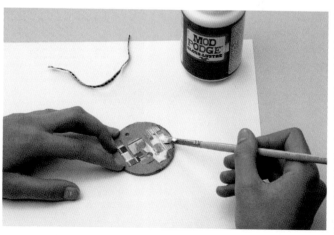

2 Carefully paint a coat of decoupage medium over the sticker word before stringing a decorative ribbon through the hole. Mount the tag to your scrapbook page.

Becoming a cheerleader after only being in this school district a year is something to be proud of!

You are a natural leader;

people are drawn to your personality!

Cheerleaders

Remember that someone will always be looking to you as an example!

Lead them in the right direction!

leader

Tamara Joyce-Wylie

Cheerleaders

An earth tone color-blocked background allows the bright red dress of the cheerleader to pop on this spread, which is definitely something to cheer about. Slender journaling strips and rub-on letters complete the layout.

She Scores!

By manipulating photos to appear black-and-white while allowing the featured cheerleader to remain in vivid color, viewers can easily locate the key figure in the pictures.

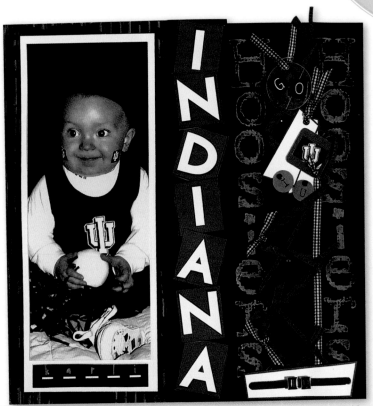

Sue Fields

Indiana

The vertical elements on this page bellow a love for a team that's climbed the ladder of victory. The helter-skelter title splits the page down the middle. On one side is an endearing enlarged portrait. On the other side is a ribbon ladder created with zig-zag strips, knotted at intersections. Charms, a safety pin, swirl clip and brads embellish the page.

Sue Fields, Photos: Jennifer Jones, Frederick's Photography

Cheerleader

A color-blocked background supports the photo of a young athlete at rest. Stitch stickers run along the seams of the paper edges. The stamped title is exuberant and playful, as are the journaling strips and blocks.

The Color Guy
The History of Cheerleading

Competitive cheerleaders and fans of those leaping, dancing, hollering, and enthusiasm-boosting athletes have Johnny Campbell to thank for introducing the sport to America. In 1898, Campbell, caught up in the excitement of a University of Minnesota football game, leapt to his feet in front of the crowd and led other spectators in a rousing version of a cheer, "Rah, Rah, Rah! Sku-u-mar, Hoo-Rah! Hoo-Rah! Varsity! Varsity, Minn-e-So-Tah!" From that one-man-show, cheerleading has expanded to include more than three million young men and women in the United States alone!

Scrapbooking Historical Pages

Capture a sense of history on sports pages that feature vintage photos of friends and family. While uniform styles and sporting equipment change as decades roll by, the sense of athletic spirit and competition remain the same. And talents that are passed from generation to generation appear and reappear, documented in cherished photos. Pages that illustrate the continuity and evolution of these talents and strengths are exciting to witness and even more exciting to scrapbook on heritage scrapbook pages.

Teresa Brada

Remember When

A modern photo joins a historical photo on this meaningful layout that represents two generations of football players. The more recent photo is matted on red textured cardstock before being mounted on a patterned paper background. The vintage photo is printed on textured cardstock and layered over patterned and mulberry papers. A faux vintage postcard, journaled ribbon, brads, a page turn, index tabs and stickers embellish the page. Metal-rimmed tags sport the players' numbers. Journaling is slipped behind one of the photos to complete the page.

Soccer Family

Soccer is the rage today and has been for years, as documented on this neat page showing a father-son love for the sport. An old newspaper story, reduced and printed on cardstock, is mounted on a patterned paper background. Photos of two different generations of soccer players (father and son) are mounted in the corners. Aging of the oversized tag helps blend it into the texture of the heritage page. The tag is slipped behind the "soccer" transparency. Ribbons, Dymo labels, and tiny paper tags embellish the layout.

Summer Fullerton

From The Color Guy
Sports heroes who made it big on the silver screen

John Wayne: Played football for Southern Cal and, when a surfing injury sidelined him, he turned his talents to acting

Johnny Weismuller: Won three Olympic gold swimming medals in 1924 and two more in 1928 before becoming "Tarzan" in the movies

Buster Crabbe: Won a gold swimming medal in 1932 before doing his own Tarzan stint and nailing the role of "Flash Gordon" in the movies

Geena Davis: Known for her role as a pro baseball player in *A League of Their Own* (as well as *Accidental Tourist* and *Thelma and Louise*), her true sport is archery, where she is known as an international competitor

Eleanor Holm: Won swimming Olympic gold in 1932 (and might have done it again in 1936 if she hadn't been caught drinking champagne and playing craps en route to the games. She was thrown off of the team) before starring in *Tarzan* movies.

Chuck Connors: Known for playing "Lucas McCain" in *The Rifleman* television show and the miniseries *Roots*, played pro basketball for the Boston Celtics and first base for both the Brooklyn Dodgers and Chicago Cubs.

John Berardino: His baseball career with the St. Louis Browns somehow (don't ask how) paved the way for him to play "Dr. Steve Hardy" on *General Hospital*.

Randall "Tex" Cob: Boxed his way out of the ring and into more than 20 movies including *Raising Arizona, Uncommon Valor* and television shows such as *Miami Vice* and *Married With Children*.

Scrapbooking as Sport

Scrapbooking doesn't involve balls, bats, skates, rackets or any other kind of sporting equipment. But like athletes, scrapbookers spend hours honing their skills. They are focused and pour their hearts into what they do. They strive to create better and better pages. Yes, scrapbooking and sports have a lot in common. Why not, just for fun, scrapbook SCRAPBOOKING as though it were an athletic experience?

Angela Moen

Confessions of a Scrapper!

A mixture of colorful patterned papers come together on this lively page detailing the life of a scrapbook enthusiast. Stitching, ribbons, buttons and brads add just the right touch of lighthearted fun to support the tongue-in-cheek journaling.

The Color Guy
Scrapbooking Your Way to Fitness

Gather your scrapbooking supplies and get fit. There's a new exercise craze across the country called Scraprobics (or there should be!) guaranteed to firm and tone while you scrapbook.

Calf refiners: Turn your calves into sculpted mounds of awesomeness without ever leaving your crafting chair. Begin by planting your feet firmly on the floor. Slowly tense your calve muscles. Lift your heels and slowly roll your feet onto demi-point. Squeeze. Release. Repeat twenty times.

Buttock builders: Turn your buns into sculpted mounds of awesomeness. Plant your feet. Identify the muscles on the right side of your tush. Squeeze those muscles. Count to five. Release. Repeat on the other side. Warning: This exercise is best to do while scrapbooking solo—doing it in public is almost certain to draw attention.

Bicep toners: Turn your arms into sculpted mounds of awesomeness. Begin by putting down your scissors and craft knife or any other sharp object. This is VERY IMPORTANT. Plant your feet. Slide your hands, palm-down, under your outer thighs halfway between your hip and knee. Gently straighten your arms and release. Repeat until you get bored.

Finger-firmers: Open and close your scissors twenty times over the course of a scrapbooking session. Squeeze a piece of polymer clay forty times before flattening or sculpting.

Disclaimer: We just made this stuff up. Do not use Scraprobics as an exercise program and please don't run with scissors.

Art Captions & Quiz Answers

Summer Golf (Pg. 7) *Maria Kress*

Whimsical elements, layers of colorful geometrics, and a rising and falling title are fun ways to convey the energy of a tike serious about his swing. The sequentially numbered photo wall shows all of the action while a title reinforces it. Ribbons, stitching and other embellishments add flare.

Practice Makes Perfect (Pg. 8) *Angela Moen*

The background of this page speaks of America's favorite pastime with stitched strips of patterned paper and red cardstock. An action photo supports an informal portrait of a young athlete. Journaling and minimal embellishments including fiber-tied tags, finish the layout.

Promise Me (Pg. 54) *Laura McKinley*

A layered background of cardstocks, vellum and patterned papers forms a platform for a sanded focal photo. Rub-ons and letter stickers form the title and a transparency journaling strip is selectively painted with "Play" before being mounted at the bottom of the page. Smaller duplicates of the focal photo are stamped with the letters of the word, "fish" and then sprinkled with embossing powder for a watery effect, before being mounted below the focal photo. A tiny altered gift book, decorated with ribbons and rub-ons, is mounted at the lower corner of the layout. A tab marks the place of a favorite quote.

I Wanna Be a Cowboy (Pg. 98) *Sherri Wright*

An old west feeling is captured on this page featuring red bandana and denim patterned paper, silver conchos, and leather straps. The leather frame, blue jean tag which is tucked behind the stencil letter "C" and hat sticker, support the rough and rugged theme. The stitched effects are created with stickers. Both the stencil "C" and title letters in "cowboy" are painted to look like suede and then distressed with ink.

Balance

A graceful ice dancer glides across a background of paper strips and a large textured paper circle. A notch is cut from the focal photo to make room for a supporting picture. Two other small photos are mounted nearby. A circle die cut, letter stickers, rickrack, a buckle, and decorative buttons add to the graceful lines.

You're Yankin' My Chain
(Sports terms that really do exist.)
Answers from quiz page 43
1. Sport or extreme martial arts
2. Skate boarding
3. Ice hockey
4. Trampoline
5. Curling
6. Fencing
7. Archery

Movie Sports Trivia
Answers from page 66
1. Crash Davis
2. A volleyball named Wilson
3. Jamaica
4. Eggs
5. The Harder They Fall
6. Carmen
7. Garden hoe

Mary-Catherine Kropinski

Index